THE ROLEX

Franz-Christoph Heel, editor

STORY

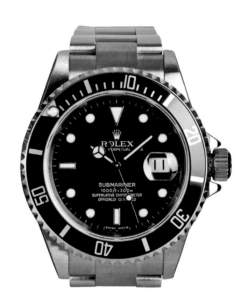

4880 Lower Valley Road • Atglen, PA 19310

Type set in ExPonto/Optima/Futura Bk BT

ISBN: 978-0-7643-4597-5
Printed in China

Published by Schiffer Publishing, Ltd.
4880 Lower Valley Road
Atglen, PA 19310
Phone: (610) 593-1777; Fax: (610) 593-2002
E-mail: Info@schifferbooks.com

For our complete selection of fine books on this and related subjects, please visit our website at www.schifferbooks.com. You may also write for a free catalog.

This book may be purchased from the publisher. Please try your bookstore first.

We are always looking for people to write books on new and related subjects. If you have an idea for a book, please contact us at proposals@schifferbooks.com.

Schiffer Publishing's titles are available at special discounts for bulk purchases for sales promotions or premiums. Special editions, including personalized covers, cor-porate imprints, and excerpts can be created in large quantities for special needs. For more information, contact the publisher.

Originally published © 2009 by HEEL Verlag GmbH, Königswinter, under the title, ROLEX. Translated by Omicron Language Solutions, LLC.

Photos:
ArmbandUhren archive, Auktionshaus Dr. Crott, Marcel Coutier, Rainer Fromm, Jörg Hajt, Martin Häußermann, Hardy Mutschler, Rolex Factory Photographs

THE ROLEX STORY

Foreword

Rolex fascinates. In little more than one hundred years, what began as an artistic concept has developed into an iconic brand, and today it is one of the most profitable watch brands in the world. There is no doubt that this is a result of successful marketing from the very beginning; just one example was the young swimmer who swam the English Channel with a Rolex on her arm and the next day found herself on the front page of the Daily Mail. However, there are also the statesmen, sports aces, and movie stars who publicly wear a Rolex as a matter of course — whether it was a gift or an item they purchased for themselves, is of secondary importance. Otherwise, the House of Rolex, supported by the Wilsdorf Foundation, has been very reserved in its press and public relations work. It is only recently that the manufacturer has opened up and granted a small number of journalists a glimpse of its inner life.

Rolex, which is publicly registered, is very likely the watch manufacturer with the highest level of vertical integration in Europe: Rolex designs its own watch cases and movements, and produces them almost completely in-house. Rolex also has the capability to manufacture its own balance springs and produce its high-quality watches in highly efficient serial production — generally, more than half a million per year. Rolex releases very few official figures, but the number of movements the company presents for inspection at the Official Swiss Chronometer Testing Institute (Contrôle Officiel Suisse des Chronomètres, COSC), is a clear indication. Here, Rolex, year after year, is far ahead of all the other prestigious Swiss watch brands.

Although a Rolex, purely objectively, is a mass-produced product, the watches bearing the crown are regarded as a luxury item worldwide. Rolex is also a favorite subject among collectors. None of this came by chance. Such continuous success for over a century cannot be explained by marketing alone; such success requires substance, which Rolex provides in the form of products with an outstanding degree of brand recognition and near-perfect quality. This fact is acknowledged — sometimes grudgingly — by the competition, and all of these features provide editors with more material for reports, new ideas, and tests. Now, you will be able to read all the most important material in this book.

I hope you enjoy reading it.

Herzlichst, Ihr

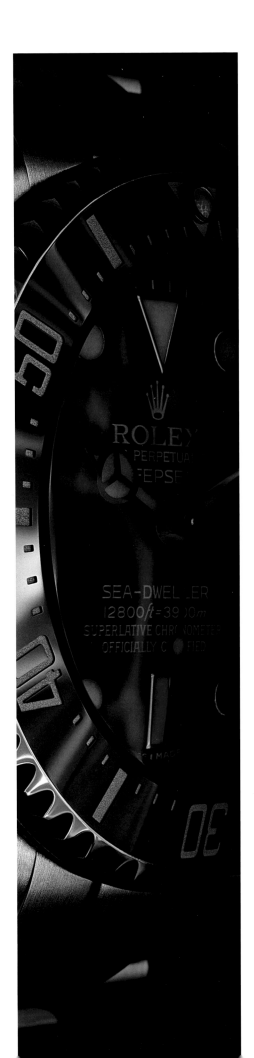

Contents

Brand and Myths

Success Story Under the Sign of the Crown

Hans Wilsdorf,
founder of the Rolex watch brand.

Prominent advertising media, ingenious product-placement — as in some "James Bond" films, and successful marketing from the very beginning are not enough to explain why Rolex has matured over some one hundred years from an art concept to an iconic brand. This has also included a good measure of substance, as the history of Rolex and its founder, Hans Wilsdorf, make clear.

Many important people wear Rolex. One is the Dalai Lama, who received his Datejust as a gift from a statesman friend. This form of PR delights the Rolex leadership ranks. There, they like to adorn themselves with reputable personalities. It has been noted with joy in Geneva that people such as Winston Churchill, Konrad Adenauer, or Charles de Gaulle publicly wore a Rolex on their arm. Now, the testimonials of this luxury brand come more from the fields of research and sports. Former champions, such as the racing driver Sir Jackie Stewart, the golfer Arnold Palmer, or skiing downhill racer Jean-Claude Killy, speak to the solvent 50-plus generation, while dynamic youth respond to tennis ace Roger Federer. They all promote a brand that has a worldwide reputation comparable to those of Mercedes-Benz and Coca Cola.

There are different views on how the name Rolex came about. The German watchmaker Hans Wilsdorf (1881-1960) of Kulmbach stated that he himself invented the name, which supposedly derives from the French "horlogerie exquise" for "exquisite watches."

Another anecdote says that a Spanish employee of Wilsdorf's created the abbreviation "Relex" from the term "Relojes excellentes" (Spanish for "excellent watches"). Neither story has been proven.

What is certain is that in 1908 Hans Wilsdorf founded Montres Rolex SA, thus laying the cornerstone for what is an unparalleled success story in this industry up till today. The Rolex founder had set himself the goal to showcase an accurate wristwatch that could compete with the then-still predominant pocket-watches. He defined the core values of the brand, which still defines its essence — highest quality craftsmanship in manufacturing and workmanship, the greatest possible precision, along with robustness and suitability for everyday wear — right up to models for all kinds of different extreme-stress usage.

Wilsdorf was more than a manufacturer; he was also a gifted salesman and a marketing expert — a craft, which, at the time, still operated/traded under the label "propaganda." He had quickly realized how you could utilize people as "testimonials," who would convey the product's message. With tremendous will-power, initiative, and a sure instinct, he put his ideas and ideals into effect.

Wilsdorf did this, despite the fact that his biography began with a great misfortune: At age twelve, he lost both of his parents in quick succession; first his mother and then his father. As a result, relatives took on the responsibility of caring for him and his two siblings; they liquidated his father's business and invested the money profitably. These relatives were the Bavarian brewer dynasty Meisel, the family from which his mother came. Why not make a good brewer of little Hans? However, nothing could be less appropriate for Wilsdorf.

Standing On His Own Feet

After his education at a boarding school in Coburg, in Bavaria, Germany, Wilsdorf completed a commercial apprenticeship with a man who ran an international artificial pearl business in Bayreuth,

Bavaria, Germany. Commercial business suited Wilsdorf. At the same time he had great interest in watch technology and foreign languages, so, at just twenty years old, he went to La Chaux-de-Fonds, in Switzerland, to the big watch export company Cuno Korten. For 80 francs a month ($89 in today's U.S. market), he handled their English correspondence, performed office work, and dealt on a daily basis with the pocket-watches that the company handled. The precision of time measurement rapidly became his obsession. Using a part of his paternal inheritance, he bought three gold pocket-watches and had their precision logged at an observatory with an accuracy certificate. He then he sold the watches at a profit.

Before he moved in 1903 to the then-center of the industrial world, London, Wilsdorf fulfilled his one-year military service in the Imperial Army of the German Reich. In 1905, he founded his own watch-trading firm together with the much older James Alfred Davis, under the name "Wilsdorf & Davis." He had to borrow some of his capital from his brother and sister because his 30,000 gold marks legacy from his father was stolen during his crossing to England.

While pocket-watches had awakened his interest and enthusiasm for the world of watches, now, above all, it was the industry's innovation — the wristwatch — that was becoming a rapidly developing market. At the Aegler watch factory in Biel, Switzerland, he bought so many high-quality small lever movements that the amount to be paid was five times the firm's capital. However, his plan bore fruit, and success proved him right. As early as 1907, the flourishing company opened a branch in La Chaux-de-Fonds. By 1908, Wilsdorf & Davis was one of the largest companies in the European watch trade and had two hundred models in its product range. The watches were sold either anonymously or with the logo of the respective dealer. Only the case was stamped with "W/D" for "Wilsdorf and Davis." This displeased their patrons, as did the fact that wristwatches at the time were almost exclusively reserved for the ladies and considered "unmanly."

Against All Odds

As a first step, Wilsdorf came up with a product name, of which he later wrote: "It was so short and yet so memorable, that there was still enough space beside it on the dial for the English dealer's name. However, especially valuable was: ROLEX sounds well, is easy to re-member, and could also be pronounced the same in all European languages." It would take some twenty years until the new name was established. Initially, Wilsdorf had used a trick: In each of the six-part boxes, only two watches were inscribed "Rolex"; later, it was three or four, making it possible to get the name established in a dealer's display window.

Of course, the young company had to provide proof of the quality of small watch movements. Could the dainty ladies' watches stand up to the respectable chronometers in men's vest pockets in terms of accu-racy? They could! In 1910, Wilsdorf had received, in Biel, a First Class certificate for a wristwatch movement with a 1" diameter (24.81 mm). In 1914, at the Kew Observatory in England, Rolex accomplished quite a feat: it had the first wristwatch honored with a Class A certificate of accuracy because it achieved the accuracy performance of a na-val chronometer. Suddenly, Wilsdorf belonged to the circle of the most prestigious watchmakers of England — and this with a wristwatch!

The watch movements were delivered from the outset by the Aegler Company, in Biel, the enterprise of Jan Aegler, and his factory, founded in 1878. Since 1881, the company had its headquarters in Rebberg, near Biel, and from 1900, was exporting ladies' wristwatches all over the world — except England (from 1913), so as not to compete with Rolex's important business partner. In 1914, the company was con-verted, under the name "Aegler SA, Rolex Watch Company," into a cor-poration. It had two hundred employees and was the exclusive supplier for the Wilsdorf & Davis Rolex Watch Company. Aegler remained an independent company until 2004, when then-President of Rolex Patrick Heiniger bought it for the princely sum of 2.5 billion Swiss francs ($2.7 billion U.S. dollars) and incorporated it into the Rolex SA.

War is Father of All Things

In relation to the wristwatch, "War is the father of all things" (in latin "Bellum omnium rerum pater est") may actually apply. The numerous British colonial wars, as well as the First World War, promoted wearing a watch on your wrist — where an officer could read it quickly and easily — to coordinate attacks by artillery and infantry.

This development brought Rolex its desired business success, although in 1919, the increase of the English import duties to 33.3 percent meant the end for the Wilsdorf & Davis Rolex Watch Company. Export activities were transferred to the Biel office; Wilsdorf himself moved with his wife to Geneva, Switzerland. In 1920, the company was renamed as "Montres Rolex SA," after Wilsdorf had detached himself from his incompatible partner. Production of the movements continued in Biel; case-making and assembling the watches in Geneva. In 1925, a brand symbol, or logo, was added to the brand name in the form of a five-pointed crown, which from 1939 up to today, adorns all Rolex watches.

The company's history is characterized by the hard struggle to perfect the wristwatch, which was always reaffirmed anew by official test certificates. The observatories of Kew, Geneva, and Besançon became the important reference points. Rolex has continued, to this day, the policy of independently testing its watches. Rolex remains the watch manufacturer with the most certified chronometers in the whole world. As early as 1968, Rolex had reached the million-level for chronometers; presently, there are likely more than 20 million Rolex-made watches with cer-tificates—and each year more than half-a-million chronometers are added.

Hermetically Sealed

Water was always a natural enemy of me-chanical watch movements. There were nev-er any waterproof pocket-watches; it wasn't until the 1920s that a case design appeared on the market, making it possible to hermeti-cally insulate the movement from external influ-ences. Rolex was an important innovator in this development. In addition to mechanical robust-ness and achieving higher accuracy performance, making waterproof watches was Wilsdorf's stated goal. This was realized by using carefully sealed case parts that were screwed to each other: a crown with a screw thread and seal, and a form-fitted crystal. A name was quickly found — "Oyster" — the oyster as a symbol of the hermetic seal. It also stands for the masterful market-ing of Hans Wilsdorf.

Wilsdorf fastened a Rolex Oyster on the wrist of a young British swimmer, Mercedes Gleitze, for her swim across the English Chan-nel, thus making it clear to the entire world that the breakthrough of creating a waterproof watch was achieved. This success was announced in a full-page ad on the front page of the Daily Mail of November 24, 1927. Suddenly, Rolex, "the wonder watch that defies the elements," was the talk of the town (see also Chapter 3, "Submariner").

Extreme athlete Mercedes Gleitze swam the English Channel with an "Oyster" on her wrist.

Early Oyster "Channel swimmer watch" (1935), Prince Brancard chronometer "Observatory quality" (1936), and Oyster Viceroy (1940) in two-tone case

As a further advertising gimmick, Rolex used small aquariums for concessionaires to display the watch to astonished window-shoppers with a goldfish swimming around it. Very quickly, however, it emerged that the screw-down crown was the weak point of the design, since it had to be opened and closed to wind the watch each day, causing considerable wear. Therefore, in 1931, Rolex developed an automatic winding mechanism with an oscillating rotor weight, which was patented in 1933. We can assert with complete justification that this revolutionized the development of the wristwatch — although only when the patent protection had expired and other manufacturers adopted the system.

Automatically Wound

The Oyster, with Reference Number 1858, was the first Rolex with the rotor mechanism. After you wear it for six hours, it will be fully wound, as the proud advertisement promised. However, the advertisement failed to state that the watch could, as before, also be wound using the crown. In 1945, the midnight-prompted jumping date display went into production. This was the birth of the "Datejust." Also, in this year, Rolex's 50,000th chronometer was certified in Biel.

The chronology of the company's achievements can still be found today on every Rolex dial: "Superlative Chronometer Officially Certified" recalls the strict testing criteria; "Oyster" the waterproof case design; "Perpetual," Rolex's development of the automatic winding mechanism, and "Datejust," the date display that jumps exactly at midnight. This represents a condensed history of a long technical development process, documented on the tiniest space.

Rolex also made watches that were luxurious, elegant, and not designed for sports: the "Prince," a square watch with hand-wound shaped movement and decentralized small second hand, was launched on the market at the end of 1928 and aimed at the world of the rich and famous — as "the Watch for Men of Distinction," according to contemporary advertising. For King George V's Silver Jubilee, four hundred watches of this type were ordered, of course, as certified chronometers (see also Chapter 5, "Prince").

The model was so successful that it remained in production for forty years and even was recently revived — it is another hallmark of Rolex that it does not unnerve its customers with hectic model changes. Meanwhile, Rolex's internal brand record is held by the "Submariner," which has been manufactured for fifty years, without becoming the least outdated.

The Foundation Model

In 1944, Wilsdorf again suffered a blow: his wife, May Florence, died. Since the marriage was childless, he transferred his shares of Montres Rolex SA to the Hans Wilsdorf Foundation. This was a wise decision regarding the continued existence of the company, as other companies that function on the foundation model have demonstrated — such as the piston manufacturer Mahle or the Bosch Company, both based in Stuttgart, Germany. From all these foundation-model companies, as in the case of Rolex, significant financial resources flow into scientific, charitable, or social projects around the world (see the box on the Rolex Foundation).

The seventieth birthday of the well-beloved patron was celebrated in 1951 with a four-day festival in Geneva — which also commemorated his fifty years of service to time-keeping, as well as twenty-five years of the Oyster watch case and twenty years of the automatic winding mechanism. Despite his advanced age, Wilsdorf still determined the company's fortunes, even though he now had two additional directors at his side. During the summer months, he lived with his second wife on the south side of Lake Geneva. Every morning, his chauffeur, Rüttimann, drove him to work in his Mercedes-Benz, the make of automobile to which he remained loyal from 1935 on.

Self-winding and with a waterproof screw-down crown, the "Oyster" was perfect from 1931. At right, an Oyster Perpetual Chronometer from 1939.

A Rolex Oyster Datejust Chronometer of 1952

After Wilsdorf's death, André J. Heiniger took over the presidency of Montres Rolex SA and the Hans Wilsdorf Foundation in 1963.

Wilsdorf's death at the age of seventy-nine in 1960 marked the end of an era. From 1963, his confidant André J. Heiniger, as president, led the fortunes of Montres Rolex SA and the Hans Wilsdorf Foundation. In 1992, André's son Patrick took over directing the business; he had to end his chairmanship at the end of 2008. With this, the company Montres Rolex SA drew a line under the "Heiniger era" after forty-five years. Over the years, the Heiniger dynasty developed Rolex into one of the most profitable companies in the watch industry. By concentrating the complete manufacturing and production process under their own roof and maintaining a very conservative product policy, the House's products gained an exemplary quality. Unperturbed by the currents on the watch market, Rolex kept to a reasonable range of models, without watches with complications, and ultimately profited from the renaissance of the mechanical watch.

The Heinigers' successor was the former finance director of Montres Rolex SA, Bruno Meier. The appointment of an established financial expert (Meier was previously head of the Swiss branch of Deutsche Bank) highlighted the importance of a prudent fiscal policy in the emerging crisis in the world of luxury watches.

From 1992 to the end of 2008, Patrick Heiniger was chairman of Montres Rolex SA.

With innovative technology and newly-structured production facilities, Rolex can calmly look forward to the next one hundred years.

Do Good: The Rolex Foundation

Companies that convert their enterprise into a foundation have two primary objectives: One, the continuance of their life's work, and secondly, they want to share a part of their success with humanity. Thus, Hans Wilsdorf determined that a portion of the profits of his company would be used to promote "knowledge and welfare for mankind."

Of particular interest is Rolex's commitment to education and training programs for fine watch-making. Behind this are elite watch-making schools in Switzerland, Japan, and the United States, which every year train twelve talented individuals in the watch industry in a two-year, intensive training course. The summit of altruism: the graduates can then freely choose their employer.

Rolex supports international cultural education through its "Awards for Enterprise." Since 1976, every two years, the Foundation has selected five individuals with a special enterprising spirit and whose projects serve to improve living condi-

tions on our planet. Particular examples of note: Gordon Sato, of Japanese-American descent, who developed an agricultural program in Eritrea, making it possible to raise mangroves in one of the driest regions of the world, and the Canadian Dave Irvine-Halliday, who, using inexpensive, more reliable, and energy-efficient lighting for homes and schools in developing countries, raised both the educational and living standards.

Of course, the Foundation also supports the Fine Arts. The "Mentoring and Protégé Arts Initiative" promotes young talents in music, dance, literature, film, theater, and the visual arts with a $50,000 scholarship, which allows the young artists to receive guidance from a luminary of their genre. As a result, Sir Peter Hall, an English theater and film director, has helped a South African launch an international career. Equally successful have been Jessye Norman, opera singer; Mario Vargas Llosa, recipient of the 2010 Nobel Prize in Literature; and Peter Sellars, American theater director — they have each taken very gifted young people under their wings.

Rolex is well-positioned for the future. A visit to several manufacturing facilities shows the Swiss firm to be a highly integrated watch manufacturer.

The Oyster Opens

In 2008, the Rolex brand celebrated its one-hundredth birthday, likely in a very relaxed way since the complete restructuring of the company has been completed. With the purchase of the movement manufacturer of Rolex in Biel and the reorganization of the Geneva assembly facilities, the company considers itself fit for the next century.

Even revolutionaries know good quality. The image of Ernesto "Che" Guevara with a Rolex Oyster on his arm went around the world, making the Cuban guerrilla fighter and politician posthumously an unofficial ambassador of the brand with the crown. Whether this was okay with Patrick Heiniger is not known; at the end, the Rolex CEO largely avoided publicity. However, judging by the more recent development of the House of Rolex, revolution seems not to be its business, but rather a calculated company policy and evolution. The goal is to attain the greatest possible vertical range of manufacture and to control costs and quality from the start. On the other hand, Rolex strives for a high degree of independence from suppliers.

This gold Rolex ladies' watch is now ready for sale. A tag reveals it is as a tested chronometer. Chronometer-testing is the rule for Rolex Oyster models.

Heiniger made a critical decision in this direction in 2004. He bought the hitherto legally- and economically-independent manufacturer Montres Rolex SA, Biel, and integrated it into Rolex SA, Geneva. This way, he killed two birds with one stone: he took control over a vitally important supplier and secured at the same time the most important export market of the House. Rolex Biel produces the automatic move-

Large glass surfaces dominate the Rolex production site in Chêne-Bourg, Switzerland. The character of the architecture reflects the product throughout: restrained, but impressive.

ment caliber 3135, together with its derivatives, which tick in different Oyster models, that have made the company great. Beyond this, Rolex Biel also has the trademark rights for the United States.

The Biel Company had belonged until then to the Borer family, descendants of Jean Aegler, with whom Rolex founder Hans Wilsdorf had made a long-term commitment to be his exclusive supplier in 1920. According to reports in Swiss business magazines, the supply contract would have expired in 2013, which could have seriously undermined the industry giant with its estimated 3.5 billion Swiss francs annual turnover ($3.8 billion U.S.). Through integration of Rolex Biel, with a purchase price of an estimated 2.5 billion Swiss francs ($2.7 billion in U.S. dollars), the flagship firm of the approximately three hundred Swiss watch brands is sailing in calmer waters. Commenting on the transfer, a Rolex spokeswoman said: "This is like an epoch-making step, which will strengthen the brand in the long-term."

The Caliber 4160 of the Yacht-Master II was one of the first watch movements incorporating the in-house made "Parachrom" spring.

Further steps included construction of new, as well as the modernization of existing, production facilities in Geneva. In 2000, after two years of construction, the location in Chêne-Bourg went into operation. There, in a production area of some 42,650-square-feet (13,000m), Rolex has concentrated all operations for development and manufacture of dials and for setting precious stones. A fully-automated, high-bay warehouse supplies just-in-time production with the appropriate materials. Redundant systems ensure that production does not stop in the event of any breakdown or mishap in a storage silo. The logistics of the other two Geneva locations also function according to this concept. Thus, construction with huge glass facades is not just an architectural model for other production facilities.

A part of the gold, which Rolex needs for cases and watch bracelets, is self-smelted: for example, the patented red gold alloy "Everose."

For example, in Geneva's Plan-les-Ouates district, in the neighborhood of Patek Philippe, Vacheron Constantin, and Piaget, Rolex produces watch cases and metal bracelets on eleven floors, five of them below ground level. This does not only include assembly, but also development, design, and quality control. Even some of the gold required for the cases and watch bands is smelted by Rolex employees

Using roof gardens, Rolex wants to restore part of the soil sealing that resulted from constructing its facilities. There are even a few vines on the roof of the building in the Geneva district of Plan-les-Ouates

— dressed in helmets and silver fireproof jackets like the legendary firefighter "Red Adair" — in its own furnace. One example is the so-called "Everose," a patented rose gold alloy made of seventy-six percent pure gold, twenty-two percent copper, and two percent platinum. This mixture keeps the reddish hue it gets from copper permanently while commercial alloys (75 percent gold, 21 percent copper, 4 percent silver) actually turn yellow after many years. The Genevans purchase the steel, however, from the Austrian manufacturer Böhler. Of course, it is of the highest quality, designated by the number 904L, and is also used for production of surgical instruments. Anyone who regularly goes diving while wearing one of the rare steel Rolexes has nothing to fear about rust.

In another area of manufacturing, oxide formation is in no way frowned upon, but rather considered desirable — in manufacturing springs. Rolex has developed itself into one of the few watch manufacturers with the know-how to produce every tiny part that has an essential role in the accuracy of a watch by themselves. Otherwise, this technology has only been mastered by its neighbors Patek Philippe, Ulysse Nardin, Lange & Söhne, and Nivarox. The company, in the Vallée de Joux, supplies the vast majority of watch manufacturers and belongs

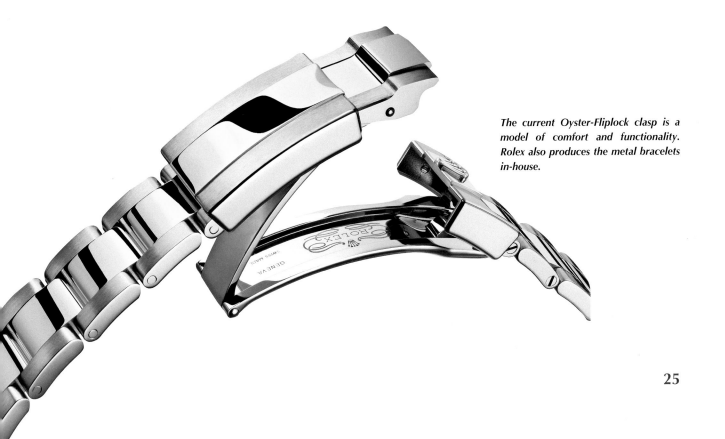

The current Oyster-Fliplock clasp is a model of comfort and functionality. Rolex also produces the metal bracelets in-house.

Fountains in front of the Rolex building in Acacias create associations to the pioneer of the waterproof sports watch.

to the Swatch Group, which also manufactures movements (ETA) and complete watches (Breguet, Blancpain, Omega, etc.). Therefore, being able to produce its own springs gives a watch manufacturer a not-to-be-underestimated strategic advantage. Not least for quality. The basis for this is laid by 280 engineers, technicians, and watchmakers in the research and development department, which, according to Rolex spokeswoman Dominique Tadion, registers five to eight patents each year.

For its so-called "Parachrom" coil spring, Rolex itself mixes the materials, which, besides iron, include niobium and zirconium. These first emerge as an approximately 11-4/5"-long (30cm), inconspicuous metal rod. Not only is the base material alloying patented, but so is the special production method, for which Rolex developed a machine that is unique worldwide and is no bigger than a clothes dryer. Roughly described, it is a vacuum chamber in which, using high voltage, sections of the rod are slowly heated and again cooled. The result is that the alloy becomes completely paramagnetic, so that the influence of magnetic fields will have no effect on the watch's accuracy. It is here that the mentioned protective oxide layer forms. Through the many rolling processes, the about 11-4/5"-long (30cm) rod is formed into a spiral spring about 118" long (3km), but just 0.002" thick (50 microns/0.05 millimeters). This is much thinner than a human hair, but, in contrast, is of the same thickness from end to end — for the perfect regulation of the accuracy for which Rolex watches are famous.

The regulator of a modern Rolex sports watch, consisting of a balance with so-called Microstella adjustment screws for rate regulation, as well as its own-brand "parachrom" spring, gets its characteristic blue color from an oxide layer.

These springs are made in the Geneva district of Acacia. Since 1965, Rolex has had its headquarters here; they were completely renovated from October 2002 to October 2006. As in Plan-les-Ouates and

Even for watches manufactured in such large quantities as Rolex, the expert hand of a watchmaker is indispensable.

Chêne-Bourg, ultra-modern glass and steel now dominate the industrial buildings where key corporate decisions are made and the entire administration is carried out. Customer service and watch assembly also have their homes here, and the movements for the "Yacht-Master II" and "Prince" models are assembled.

Everything runs based on an extreme division of labor. The Caliber 4160 movement for the regatta watch, "Yacht-Master II," passes through about sixty different workstations and, at each workstation, up to eight different assembly operations are performed. Although some one hundred people are sitting at the long work tables, a concentrated silence dominates. There is little to hear except the hum of the small electric screwdrivers and the quiet clacking of Rolex's specially-designed transport system. This is a dust-proof plastic container, which takes the movements from the first stages of production to final inspection — of course, provided with barcodes, so that each item can be tracked during the production progress. This area can only be entered through air locks and only wearing special shoes: visitors are given overshoes — and lab coats. The work here is done under clean-room conditions, with continuous positive pressure in the production hall to ensure that no speck of dust can penetrate.

More than 613,000 watches were produced in this way in 2006. The company did not itself provide this figure, but it was published by the Swiss Chronometer Testing Office, which tests watch movements for their accuracy. For many watch manufacturers, such testing is the exception, but for Rolex it is the rule. According to press spokeswoman Dominique Tadion, some 6,000 people are employed at the four Swiss locations. By comparison, A. Lange & Söhne, with 450 employees, makes about 5,500 watches per year. Granted, the comparison is somewhat flawed, as a Rolex — with the exception of the chronographs Daytona and Yacht-Master II — displays essentially only time and date, while Lange watches are usually equipped with complicated additional functions. However, Rolex's orientation is clear: mass production of the highest quality.

Here you can look in vain — contrary to some preconceptions — for any un-staffed production lines. You will also find just as few of the graying watchmakers that so many Swiss and Saxony luxury watch brands like to promote in their publicity. Whoever purchases a Rolex, must get used to the idea that they are just not simply assembled by their personal watchmaker in some romantic farmhouse. Instead, there are many people — of whom only a few are watchmakers — working in cool, multi-story functional buildings so that a Rolex can later tick reliably on its owner's wrist.

History of
the Models

Always in Good Form

Probably no watch design has shaped the image of the classic sports watch than the Rolex Oyster. The Submariner primarily, but also the GMT-Master and the Explorer, characterize the "tool watch"-type in their different designs: high-quality watches for the most varied profile of requirements that will function reliably at great heights, at extremely low or high temperatures, in deep water, or in extremely strong magnetic fields. After these, came the chronographs, which, in a world increasingly dominated by speed, made it possible to exactly record even the smallest unit of time.

Rolex Prince of 1935 with characteristic divided dial; right, a very early Prince hand-wound movement, which can be adjusted in six positions "for all climates.

The Rolex brand became popular in the late 1920s with the "Prince" model, an elegant rectangular watch with two-part dial. The decentralized second hand had a circular scale equally as large as the hour- and minute-hand time display. From 1929, the watch was offered in different case styles, including the "Railway," with stepped sides, or as the "Brancard," with a "waisted" case. These styles also came in various precious metal combinations. It was powered by the shaped movement Caliber T.S. Ref. 300, with the dimensions 3/5" x 1-1/5" (16.9 x 32.7mm). Over the years, it has been manufactured in different styles: one style came with a protecting bridge for the balance wheel; another version with jumping hours. As a rule, the movement was regulated to chronometer standard. This differentiated it from the other "off-the-shelf" movements. The producer Aegler also delivered to other manufacturers, such as Gruen and Alpina — a circumstance that makes it easy today for counterfeiters to produce

In 2003, Rolex presented an anniversary Submariner, to celebrate the 50th anniversary of this successful model.

Rolex Oyster Perpetual "Bubble Back" with covered band lugs ("hooded lugs").

The "Kew A" Caliber was developed at the end of the 1940s specially for chronometer competitions.

new "Princes." Collectors should, accordingly, be careful about any too "reasonable" offers. In 2005, Rolex presented a contemporary reinterpretation of this model, of course, chronometer-certified with hand-wound movement (see also Chapter 5, "Dignified Elegance").

While hand-wound movements were used in the early shape watches, as well as for chronographs and the "pre-Oyster" models, the waterproof "Oyster" was soon manufactured with the Perpetual Caliber, exclusively made by Aegler in Biel for Rolex; a patent was granted for its bilaterally winding automatic rotor in 1933. These early automatic models can thank, for their posthumously-acquired nickname "Bubble Back," their bulbous case backs, which allowed space for the rotor. Even with their elegantly integrated band lugs, the new watches were differentiated from other round models, which, with soldered wire clips to fasten the watchband, were still very reminiscent of converted pocket-watches. The "Hooded Bubble Back," which came on the market in the summer of 1938 with hooded band lugs, was the first bi-colored model, offered in steel and gold. This was also the debut of the metal bracelet, typical for Rolex, which created an optical unity with the watch. Up until present-day, it has shaped the lasting visual and tactile impression of the sports watch line.

Rugged and Sporty

As early as 1936, Rolex developed a waterproof watch for the Italian Navy for the Florence-based company Panerai. The first prototypes for the "Radiomir" were actually made by Rolex. However, the big success story of the brand began in 1953 with the "Submariner" diving watch, which was preceded by the "Turn-O-Graph," a so-called "tool watch" with bilateral rotating bezel, that was advertised by Rolex as a simple chronograph.

On his first ascent of Mt. Everest, Sir Edmund Hillary wore an Oyster, as the middle picture shows. In the 1930s, Rolex developed and produced diving watches for the Panerai Company.

In 1953, the Explorer was introduced; in 1954, it was the GMT-Master, with dual time zone and an additional 24-hour hand, and the "Milgauss," which can withstand magnetic fields up to 1000 Gauss. The "Day-Date," introduced in 1956, with its weekday and date displays, provides important information for the businessman. The simpler "Datejust," whose date indicator jumps exactly at midnight, was, from the start, also available as a ladies' watch, and Rolex set its entire ambition on having the delicate watch movements also be certified as a chronometer — no easy task!

In 1961, Rolex presented the Cosmograph Daytona; in 1971, the Sea-Dweller 2000 (waterproof for 2,000 feet/610m); in 1980, the Sea-Dweller 4000 (to 4,000 feet/1,220m); and in 1983, the GMT-Master II. Likewise, in the 1970s, appeared the Explorer II; specially intended for cave explorers, it has a 24-hour display. In 1992, a new product name was created with the "Yacht-Master," while the "Air King" model, an inexpensive Oyster without date-display, is one of the longest-manufactured models. Many of these models are still in production today, being constantly improved, but for the layman, often barely distinguishable from the original models. The "Milgauss," whose first production cycle ended in 1988, has been available again since 2007 in a revised version.

From 2005, the contemporary, new interpretation of the Prince.

Advertising

Early on, Rolex understood that it was important to win prominent customers — whether athlete, scientist, artist, adventurer, or mountaineer — for the brand. The most successful auto-racing driver of the 1930s, Mercedes-Benz' own racing driver Rudolf Caracciola, wore a Rolex chronograph at the starting line, as did the "fastest man in the world," speed record-holder Sir Malcolm Campbell, and world-class golfers Arnold Palmer, Jack Nicklaus, and Gary Player. The chronographs of skier Jean-Claude Killy and actor Paul Newman are still today associated with the names of their wearers by collectors.

A Rolex was also there during the first ascent of the 29,029-foot Mount Everest in 1953 by Sir Edmund Hillary and Tenzing Norgay and, in 1960, for the dive of the Trieste, when Jacques Piccard descended to a depth of 35,813 feet in the Pacific. For the many-varied sports watches family, a base automatic movement was generally used; this was modified according to how it would be used: for magnetic field protection, second time zones, 24-hour display, and so forth. This development began in 1950 with the Caliber 1030, which had a diameter of 1-1/10" (28.5mm) and a height of 1/5" (5.85mm). The oscillation frequency was a moderate 18,000vph. The movement had twenty-five jewels and screw balance with timing washers, a Breguet overcoil spring, and chronometer regulation. The Caliber 1530 fol-

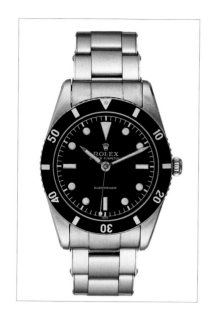

Rolex Oyster Perpetual Submariner, the original 1953 model; below, the automatic Caliber 3135 is currently used in most Oyster men's models.

In the hull of the Jacques Piccard's submarine, the Trieste, a special Oyster, with reinforced case and glass dome, reached the lowest point of the Pacific in the Mariana Trench, 38,813 feet below sea level.

lowed in 1957, with the same diameter, but twenty-six stones. Calibers 1520 and 1580 were derived from this movement in 1963, with the vibration count increased to 19,800-vph. The screw balance, with two Microstella adjustment screws, used in the Caliber 1555 is also a derivative of Caliber 1530.

A completely new movement was presented under the Caliber number 3035 (1-1/10" diameter/28.5mm, height 1/5" or 6.35mm) in 1977. It had twenty-seven jewels, and the vibration frequency now amounted to 28,800vph. The last development stage in this series is the Caliber 3135, presented in 1990, which again had been improved in many details. This conservative model policy is reflected in the quality: the sophisticated technology is a guarantee for the unconditional reliability and excellent rate values of Rolex watches.

A World Apart

Chronographs have always played a special role among Rolex sports watches. These are not only much-sought after, in-demand as new watches (especially the versions in stainless steel cases, always kept to low numbers), but they are also historical models that achieve premium prices at auction — up to twenty times the initial retail price.

The early Rolex chronographs with single push-piece control (from approximately 1930) were equipped with the 13-ligne VZ or the 10-1/2-ligne pillar or control wheel Caliber Valjoux 69. These were, corresponding to the contemporary taste, petite watches with a diameter between 1-1/10" and 1-1/5" (28, 32mm). The watches were only first made larger, with the replacement of the VZ caliber, by the Valjoux 22 (14 lignes, corresponding to 1-1/5" or 32mm movement diameter), and, in addition to the traditional round cases for chronographs, square cases were also used. Impressively sized at 1-7/10" (44mm), even by today's standards, was the rare drag indicator chronograph with the Caliber Valjoux 55 VBR.

The new "Daytona" cosmograph of 2000, in yellow gold, with its own Caliber 4130 (opposite page).

39

An early Rolex hand-wound chronograph from around 1935.

After the Valjoux 22 and 23, the Valjoux 72 followed in around 1948, which was, until the 1980s, to power most Rolex chronographs and their calendar-watch derivative, the "cosmograph" (initially without the addition of "Daytona"), right up to the last hand-wound Daytona (references 6265 and 6263). In the gold version, both in fourteen and eighteen carats, the watch with the Caliber 727 was offered for the first time as a certified chronometer. As Valjoux 72C, with month, weekday, and date display, the movement also came into use as the so-called "Pre-Daytona." The Reference 81806, with moon phase, came onto the market at the beginning of the 1950s and was made only in "homeopathic doses" (i.e., too low to work); today, it's exorbitantly expensive, although the Valjoux 88 used was also installed by other manufacturers.

The chronograph "Jean-Claude Killy" (1954), named for its prominent wearer, the French skiing ace.

With a case diameter of 1-1/2" (40mm) and a 13-ligne automatic movement, based on the Zenith 400 ("El Primero"), Rolex presented in 1988 the first automatic chronograph in its history. The balance in the Rolex caliber 4030 oscillated — in contrast to the Zenith base movement — with reduced frequency (28,800 instead of 36,000 vibrations) for better oil retention and to improve accuracy; nevertheless, all models were now certified as chronometers. For the first models, 50 to 200 km/h was sufficient for the engraved tachometer scale on the bezel; later, it became 60 to 400 km/h.

In 2000, with the chronograph Caliber 4130, Rolex presented for the first time a completely self-developed piece. The chronograph, controlled by the intermediate wheel, was made flatter than its predecessor and also has a larger power reserve (72 hours). The modern design has a balance bridge and a vertical friction clutch, which prevents a jump of the starting second hand and also makes continuous wear-free operation of the chronograph possible.

The legendary Daytona "Paul Newman,"
here in a 1960 version.

Collected Crowns

Rolex's fundamentally solid design, its global, smoothly-functioning service, and, last but not least, its brand image ensure that the watch brand has a loyal and large following among collectors. This book gives the author of that time the opportunity to present his current assessments: Stefan Muser, owner of the Dr. Crott Auction House in Manheim, Germany.

As with many watch-trends of the late 1980s and early 1990s, the passion for collecting Rolex's got its current character from Italy. At the time, Italian "street traders" — after the first rumors emerged that production of the old "cosmographs" (with manual winding base Valjoux 72 movement) would end — bought up the stocks of this not particularly sought-after model all over Europe. This immediately sent prices soaring; Muser states: "That was only the beginning. Especially in the past two years, prices have literally gone through the roof." Now, the situation has somewhat normalized, according to the assessment of this expert on antique watches. Thus, at his auction in November 2009, he had a gold Daytona (Reference 6265), with a gold bracelet, in the catalog, with an estimated price between 23,000 and 45,000 euro ($31,000–$60,000 U.S. dollars). This horrendous price range will be explained here to the uninitiated. The lower value is the seller's "pain threshold," i.e., those persons who put the watch up for auction; the upper value is that which, in the auctioneer's experience, is an attainable price.

The Reference 8171 moon phase-calendar automatic watch, manufactured between 1949 and 1952; Italian collectors also know this watch as the Padellone. It costs between 25,000 and 30,000 euros ($33,000–$40,000 U.S. dollars).

Rolex GMT-Master, Ref. 6542, Cal. 1030, 1-1/2" (38mm), from around 1958. Automatic with 24-hour display, red/black date display, and Bakelite bezel — with its original certificate. Estimated price 17,000–20,000 euros ($23,000–$27,000 U.S. dollars).

It is not possible to give an exact estimate of what price a watch will fetch. Especially with Rolex watches, collectors often focus on details, tiny special features, and rare (limited) versions. Marginal factors can make a considerable difference in price, many thousands of dollars. A manual-winding "Daytona" (offered in the References 6265, 6264, 6263, 6262, 6241, 6240, and 6239) with a rare blank-seeming dial — reverently called the "Paul Newman" by collectors because this is the watch he once wore in a movie — costs a good double the amount of its technically-identical sister models. Such a model (Reference 6262) was also to be found in the catalog of the November 2009 Dr. Crott auction, with an estimated price of between 35,000 and 50,000 euros or $47,300–$68,800 U.S. dollars (including the original case, shipping carton, additional steel bezel with tachymeter scale, instruction manual, and a Rolex service invoice). "Normal" manual-winding Daytonas are, according to Muser, currently to be had for about 15,000 to 20,000 euro ($20,200–$27,000 U.S. dollars).

Rolex chronograph, Ref. 6238, Cal. 72, 1-2/5" (36mm), from about 1961. Rolex made 3,600 pieces of the Reference 6238 — in comparison to current models, a limited edition. This so-called "Pre-Daytona" costs between 40,000 and 60,000 euros ($54,000–$81,000 U.S. dollars).

Among the Pre-Daytona watches, the Oyster chronographs without the sophisticated place names, it is what insiders call the "Jean-Claude Killy," Reference 6236 with full calendar and steel bracelet, makes collectors' hearts beat faster and achieved top prices at auctions. Muser estimates up to 80,000 to 90,000 euro ($108,000–$121,000 U.S. dollars) for such a watch. Among other sports watches, like the

Submariner or GMT-Master, more and more it is the early models without crown protectors that are in demand. Muser states: "The GMT was undervalued until now; in the meantime, with a Bakelite bezel and without crown protectors, it has become the dream of many Rolex collectors." Accordingly, he evaluates such a model, which was presented to him with a distinct patina, at 17,000 to 20,000 euro ($23,000–$27,000 U.S. dollars).

Intrinsic worth is often not decisive for Rolex collectors; value is repeatedly determined by appearance. Thus, if the lettering for "Submariner" is in red, this means a significantly higher price. When it is a matter of a "Sea-Dweller" with the imprint "COMEX" (for the company that became a pioneer of industrial deep-sea diving with its oxygen-helium mixture) and if the watch has the appropriate documentation, the price can break through the $100,000 barrier. Even little things — such as, if a "Submariner's" depth indicator is marked first in feet or in meters — is valued by collectors; these watches are distinguished as "feet first" and "meter first." A Submariner with a blue-gray bezel instead of a black one, a "Paul Newman" with a red dial, apostrophized in insider circles as the "Spirit of Japan," or an early Turn-O-Graph or an original Milgauss — all these are (provided that they are authentic) models getting extremely high prices and the trend keeps rising.

Rolex cosmograph Daytona — the so-called "Paul Newman" — Ref. 6262, Cal. 727, 1-2/5" (36mm), around 1969, estimated value 35,000 to 50,000 euros ($47,300–$68,800 U.S. dollars).

Instruments for Your Wrist

The Diving Watch

The Submariner, often apostrophized as the "mother of all diving watches," has also proven itself in diving watch tests.

The year 1953 saw the debut of a new model of the Rolex Oyster family specifically designed for the requirements of professional divers. The most important new feature of this watch, waterproof to 328 feet (100m), was a rotating ring around the outer edge of the crystal, which made it possible to mark and note the dive and decompression time periods. The Rolex Submariner was born, and with it a new category of watch.

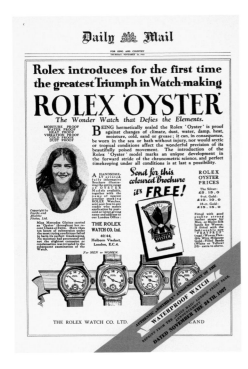

With a full-page ad on the front-page of the London Daily Mail, Rolex touted its waterproof watches. The day before, swimmer Mercedes Gleitze had swum the English Channel with a Rolex Oyster on her arm.

One of the first waterproof Rolex Oysters from 1926.

Waterproof watches were already a house specialty from the mid-1920s. Not without reason, Rolex founder Hans Wilsdorf named the rugged, stainless steel case, with the elongated body and round glass-retaining ring, after the oyster, the symbol of perfect reticence.

With its large screw-down back, a screw-down crystal-retaining ring, as well as a screw-down crown, the "Oyster" had set the standard for all future waterproof watches. "The wonder watch that defies the elements," ran the *London Daily Mail* headline on November 24, 1927, next to the photo of Channel swimmer Mercedes Gleitze and a selection of four Rolex "Oyster" watch models. Wilsdorf had long been working for this moment, and when the courageous young woman made possible this spectacular entrance for the Oyster, he pounced: for 40,000 Swiss francs ($44,000 U.S. dollars), he secured the front-page of the million-circulation daily newspaper and made his brand famous overnight.

An ancestral gallery of Submariners: At left, the Reference 6204 from 1953, still without side protectors for the crown; center, the Reference 5512, (1959) as it was made, without alterations, over several decades; at right, finally, a Submariner Date from 1983.

With the perfecting of the automatic watch movement by means of the rotor-flywheel, Rolex engineers succeeded in making another step towards sturdy and problem-free wristwatches at the beginning of the 1930s. The watch movement, which performed its service without outside intervention and got its energy right from the movement of the forearm, was an important requirement for the long-term quality of the watch, since the crown screw thread and the case tubes were largely saved from wear and were generally eliminated as a source of problems.

The relatively small Oyster models (usually less than 1-3/10" or 33mm in diameter), also called the "Bubble Back" because of their curved case backs, achieved great commercial success in the 1930s and '40s. The automatic version, "Oyster Perpetual," rapidly outstripped the manual-winding styles, and Rolex became synonymous with waterproof automatic watches, also famous for their chronometer-standard accuracy. As a result, even the most elegant and dainty Rolex watches were considered genuine sports watches in their time, although we now have a different image of sports watches. However, this image still first got its character from Rolex.

Such an item as an over-the-counter diving watch for professional use did not exist at the beginning of the 1950s. Professional divers used mostly military watches in their work — clunky devices with thick crystals and pocket-watch movements or just plain timers. These timepieces had little in common with "wearable" wristwatches.

Professional Equipment

In the 1950s, for the first time, Rolex equipped an Oyster Perpetual with a rotating bezel and called the watch, with the Reference 6202, the "Turn-O-Graph." This was the first model in the family of "professional watches" because, with its clear functionality, it was focused on users who required a means for ascertaining time intervals, but for whom a chronograph — which Rolex definitely had, though not in a waterproof design — was too expensive or, due to its technology, too delicate.

The rotating bezel of the Turn-O-Graph had a 60-minute scale and a luminous triangular zero marker, which was set on the tip of the minute hand, and, thus, helped measure shorter time intervals. The dial ring had neither a lock nor any other guard against accidental turning, which, by the way, could be done in both directions. The screw-down crown, however, already had the "Twinlock" seal, which, even if improperly screwed on, kept watertight to 164 feet water depth (50m).

The slightly later follow-up model, introduced with the Reference 6204, was explicitly intended for use underwater, which even then bore on the dial the name "Submariner" — initially without a depth indicator. In its birth year, 1953, the Submariner still had the normal Oyster case with screw-down Twinlock crown, approved, however, by Rolex for 328 feet diving depth (100m) diving depth. The generous layout of the hour markers and luminous hands ensured good readability even in conditions with little light.

With this, the Geneva brand gave professional divers, for the first time, the possibility to buy a professional timepiece tailored to their needs at a watch dealer. Using the rotating bezel, it was possible to highlight diving and decompression times and to note and read them at a glance. This important feature of the "diving bezel" was later laid down as an essential part of a diving watch in many standards and military.

Quick Evolution in a Few Steps

The Submariner got its characteristic face with the "Mercedes star" on the hour hand with the introduction of Reference 6536 in the mid-1950s. This model already had an accurate scale for the first fifteen minutes on the rotating bezel, as was later required by the various national standards for diving watches.

On its fiftieth birthday, Rolex issued this Submariner model with the additional notation LV (Lunette Verde, French "green bezel"). It is also often called the "frogmariner" and is, today, a sought-after collector's item.

The Reference 5512, in production since 1959, was the first to have a case with side guards for the screw-down crown. The case diameter was increased from 1-2/5″ to 1-3/5″ (37-40mm), and beyond this, Rolex now guaranteed it to be waterproof at 656 feet (200m) down. The Calibers of the 1500 family, modified in many areas, replaced the veteran design with 9-3/4 lignes.

The newly designed, non-slip rotating bezel had an "Auto Lock" system to prevent accidental turning or twisting: To adjust the dial number ring, you had to press it against the case; after release, it locked again.

This model finally became standard equipment for professional divers in both civilian and military fields and remained, with only small alterations, in production until 1991. Thus, for example, in 1969, the Submariner Date (Reference 1680) was introduced, the first time a Submariner was offered in a gold case. In 1979, the plexiglas was exchanged for a sapphire crystal, increasing the waterproof range to 984 feet (300m). At the end of the 1980s, the Reference 14060 finally succeeded to the Submariner legacy — with unidirectional rotating bezel, screw-down Triplock crown, and the (provisional) last evolutionary step of the automatic caliber 3000.

In diving watch tests, the Submariner scored in both day and night with its outstanding readability.

Formative Influence

Being a sturdy professional watch available in normal watch stores already ensured broad distribution of the Rolex Submariner in the 1960s. After the sports and recreational divers, sailors, and motorboat captains discovered the qualities of the diving watch, it was not long until other amateur athletes were taking note of the sturdy, low-maintenance, and reliable timepieces. Film and television heroes like Sean Connery, Roger Moore, and Paul Newman gladly wore these "professional watches," and made the Submariner popular in their own way. In collector circles, the early models (without crown side guards) were sometimes also known as "James Bond" Submariners.

The Rolex Submariner fit like no other watch in the active lifestyle of the 1960s and '70s and numerous sister models, from the Yacht-Master, to the GMT-Master, and, finally, the Sea-Dweller, followed in the same niche. In its advertisements, Rolex even encouraged private and civilian customers to buy the basically highly-specialized watches with the motto "What's right for the professionals, can only be a good buy for you."

Photos like these document the leak-proof test, which the diving watches had to undergo in Germany's alpine Lake Walchen.

The Submariner is popularly purchased in a material combination of steel and gold. Rolex calls this mix Rolésor.

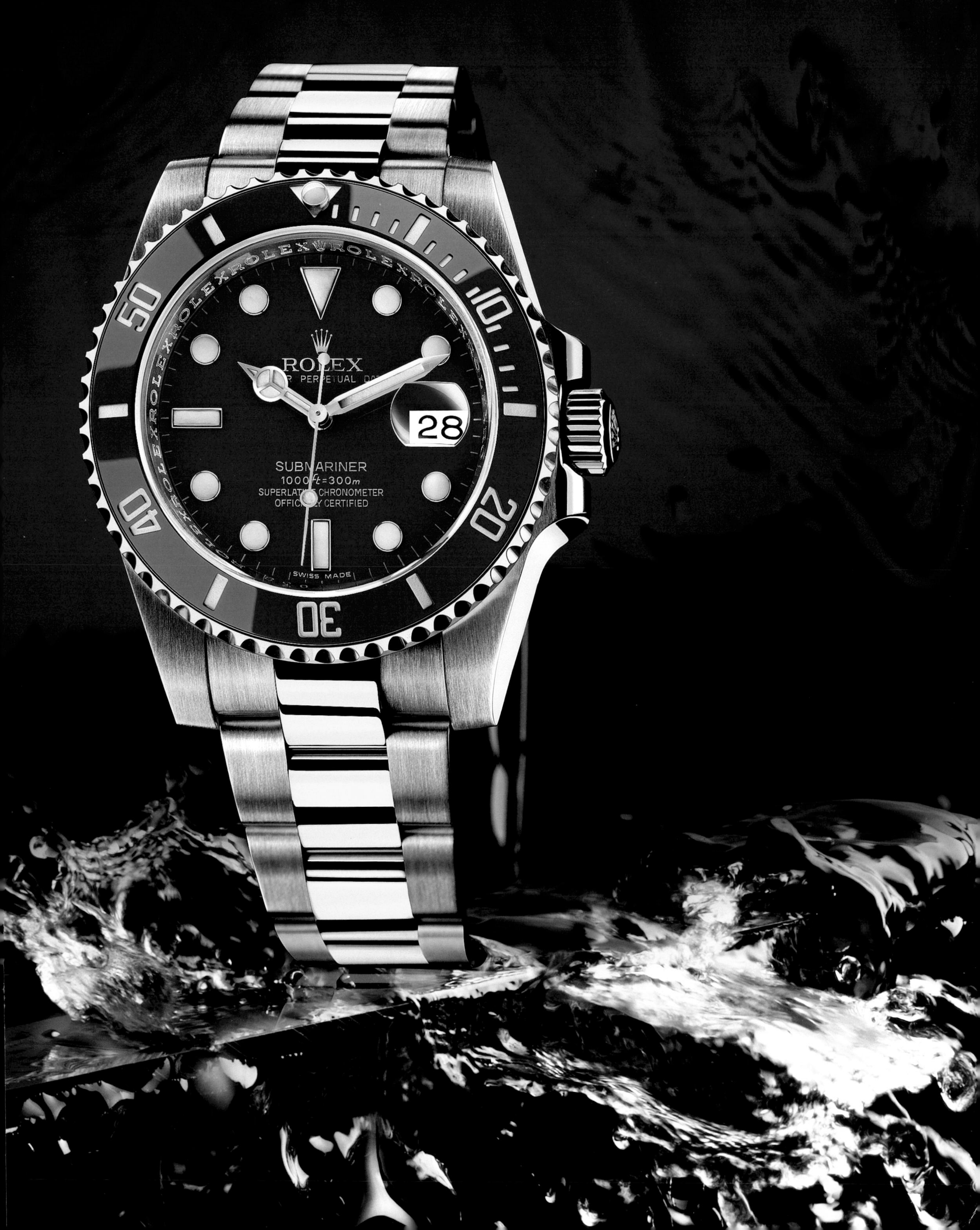
ROLEX
SUBMARINER
1000ft=300m
SWISS MADE
28

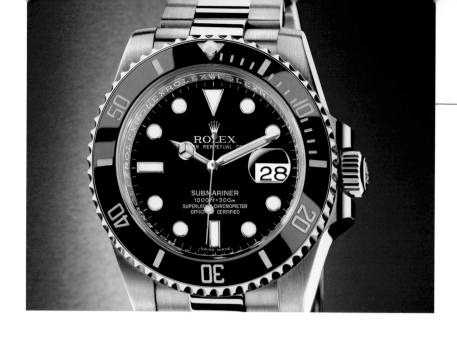

For many people, the epitome of a luxury watch: the Submariner Date in gold with gold bracelet. It represents approximately the equivalent value of a mid-size car.

Speaking of bargains: Since professional Rolex watches were never any special deal in terms of price — although 1960s prices can now reduce you to tears — owning a Submariner had not only a sporty but also a luxurious aspect. The aura of this "luxury sports watch" persists up to today, even though there have long been more luxurious, exclusive, and, incomparably, more expensive sport watches on the market. The logical evolution of its appearance, the unsurpassed readability of its displays, and the impressive functionality of the features all ensure the Submariner the status of an archetype among diving watches.

In fact, this watch just cannot be improved — at most, it is to be complemented. For its versions in gold or steel/gold ("Rolésor") or a real anniversary edition for the 50th anniversary — with a green bezel. Happy Birthday, Submariner!

Submariner in Field Trials: It Dives

In autumn 2008, the editors of (German) watch and diving sport magazines put fifteen diving watches of all price ranges under the microscope. They had to prove themselves both in the laboratory and in actual diving. For this, they went diving in Lake Walchen, to a depth of 164 feet (50m).

No question that the Rolex Submariner is one of the party. In the end, Dietmar Fuchs, unterwasser (underwater) editor-in-chief and watch connoisseur, found it to be a phenomenon: "Most people who earn money by diving wear this watch." This is why the Submariner has the image of the "mother of all diving watches." However, that, for Fuchs, is too much praise. Although Rolex, like Blancpain, already presented a rotating diving bezel in 1953, at that time it was only the Blancpain watch that was unidirectional. Rolex added this security detail only much later.

For Fuchs, the Submariner is undoubtedly a very good watch, but: "I find the Sea-Dweller DeepSea more interesting because, with this watch, Rolex took much more consideration about the requirements of divers." For example, he cites the integrated helium release valve. The titanium case back and the bezel with scratch-resistant ceramic inlay are advantages the new Sea-Dweller has compared to the Submariner. Watch connoisseurs also appreciate the Sea Dweller having the in-house-produced "Parachrom" hairspring and much-improved clasp. In practice, however, the Submariner has a clear advantage: it is definitely easier to obtain.

It also went through the field tests without weak points. It runs both at plus 20 degrees Celsius (68°F) and at 4 degrees Celsius (39.2°F) [the temperature at 164ft./50m depth] within chronometer standards (+0.4 seconds/day, -1.0 seconds/day). It completed the leak-proof test masterfully and its readability, both above and below water, was praised by the testers, which is why Fuchs, in the selection his personal favorite, was governed mainly by subjective impressions, knowing full-well that he would provoke reactions: "In my rating system, soft factors such as image and history decide the victor. For this reason, Blancpain, Doxa, and Rolex stand at the top of the podium. The second place is shared by Sinn U2, Omega, and IWC, and on the third land Panerai, Mühle, and Oris."

At the end, there is still a contradiction. As Fuchs asserted even while entering the tests: "No one today needs a watch for diving anymore. Not in times of organized Easy-Diving and certainly not since there are diving computers." At the conclusion of the test, however, he frankly admitted: "While diving, I always keep my watch on my arm." Grinning, Fuchs adds: "I'm afraid that it might be stolen."

Rolex Oyster Perpetual Submariner Date

Movement: Automatic Rolex Caliber 3135, diameter 1-1/10" (28.5mm), height 1/5" (6mm); 31 jewels, 28.800 vph
Functions: Hours, minutes, central second hand; date
Case: Stainless steel, diameter 1-1/2" (40mm), height 1/2" (12.5mm); unidirectional diving rotating bezel; sapphire crystal; screw-down crown; waterproof to 30 bar
Bracelet: Stainless steel with folding clasp and diving extension
Price: When introduced, 4,590 euros ($6,190.53 U.S. dollars today)

In 2001, the German magazine Arm-bandUhren (Wristwatches) presented the Sea-Dweller together with other extreme-diver watches, such as the *Hublot Super Professional (right)* and the *Sinn 403 Hydro (top)*.

In the Rapture of the Deep

From 1971 to 2008, Rolex manufactured the extreme diving watch, the Sea-Dweller, virtually unaltered. The first generation Sea-Dweller was presented in 2001 as a "no. 1 topic," together with other diving extremists.

Diving professional: This watch can withstand more than any diver.

"Your watch can withstand just as much as you can" Rolex once advertised the House's especially robust watches. For the Sea-Dweller, the counter-question must be allowed: Can you withstand what your watch can? A rather rhetorical question because even the first Sea-Dweller touts a pressure resistance to 4,000 feet (1,220m) water depth.

Before Gerhard Claußen, editor of Arm-bandUhren (Wristwatches), took a close look at the Sea-Dweller and its six peers (Breitling Colt Super Ocean, Hublot Super Professional, IWC Aquatimer Panerai Luminor Submersible, Sinn 403 Hydro, and TAG Heuer Specialist 1000m/3,281 ft.), he discussed the general theme of diving watches:

"The 20th century brought us — among many other more or less welcome changes — the technical capability to explore the underwater world in a way unheard of before. Diving has indeed not just become a mass popular sport, but sports divers are an interested target audience for advertising of watch companies."

The Rolex folding clasp bears the brand logo on its back and both "wings" are imprinted with the company name. The case back is covered with a foil to protect the lid from scratching before sale. Since this foil is also copied on Rolex imitations, today it is made forgery-proof with a kind of watermark.

Careful selection when buying a diver's watch is, therefore, all the more necessary because, as with many other technical products and watches in general (in particular diving watches), it is difficult to separate the wheat from the chaff. Some "diving watches" may be waterproof, but many more are not. Even with high-quality watches, it behooves the buyer to use due diligence when planning any stay underwater: they should check the waterproof quality of their watch regularly.

Indeed, the electronic age has already created the battery-powered, microprocessor-controlled diving computer, which provides, in addition to immersion time, lots of other important information for people underwater. However, this has not meant any end for the development, production, and sales of mechanical diving watches. One reason, of course, is that this style of watch goes perfectly in the drawer of the "manly man." However, there are also purely practical reasons: if the electronics should suddenly fail for lack of energy or other adverse circumstances, you can still rely on good old mechanics" — and this certainly goes, specifically, for a Rolex diving watch.

Sea-Dweller

No other watch brand earned a reputation earlier and more consistently to make reliable watches both on land and in the watery element as Rolex. The Geneva manufacturer can thank its reputation to not only the most often-mentioned woman in the history of watch-making — the Englishwoman Mercedes Gleitze, who in 1927, with a Rolex on her wrist, swam the English Channel, even at its narrowest point at least 98,425 feet wide (30k) — but up to this day, various sports personalities repeatedly reaffirm that they rely on the resilience and precision of a Rolex in their outstanding achievements.

The aura of a heavy-duty wristwatch is thanks to the unique design of the so-called Oyster case, which is milled from one piece of steel or gold (see also Chapter 2, "History of the Models"). These special case shells are closed with a screw-down case back, which can only be opened using special tools. The watch front is hermetically sealed with a special hardened sapphire crystal, as are the winding stem bores by a screw-down winding crown with several seal rings.

Left: An equalization valve (usually referred to as a "helium valve") is set opposite the crown. During a prolonged stay in the helium-containing air of diving stations, this allows gases that had diffused through the case material into the interior to escape during decompression.

Right: The movement: Rolex-crafted Caliber 3135, diameter 1-1/10" (28.5mm); height 1/5" (6mm), bilaterally winding automatic, 31 jewels, regulation (without index pin and regulator) by Micro-stella adjustment screws, official chronometer with COSC certificate.

Rolex Sea-Dweller

Reference No.: 16600
Movement: Rolex Caliber 3135, diameter 1-1/10" (28.5mm), height 1/5" (6mm); 31 jewels; automatic, 28,800 vph; power reserve 46 hours
Functions: Hours, minutes, seconds, date
Dial: Black lacquered, imprinted minute track, luminescent, applied index markers, steel hands ("pencil" style) with luminous coating.
Case: Diameter 1-1/5" (39.5mm), height 3/5" (14.8mm), steel, matt and polished; sapphire crystal, uni-directional rotating adjustment ring with minute-interval ratchet; screw-down back, screw-down crown, waterproof to 4,000 feet (1,220m)
Bracelet: Stainless steel, matt and polished, folding clasp with safety catch
Special Features: Gas pressure escape valve; official chronometer with certificate
Price: When introduced, € 3,208.35 / DM 6,275 ($4,327 U.S. dollars today/DM $8,463)

All Oyster models function effortlessly to water depths of 328 feet (100m). For a number of "Oysters," however, much greater depths are also no problem. The "Sea-Dweller" belongs to the Submariner collection, which was first launched in 1953, and thus is among the few genuine classics — both among the Rolex time-pieces and diving watches overall. The "Rolex Oyster Perpetual Date Sea-Dweller," the full name of this waterproof lady, is generally available in the already-considered characteristic design with black dial and an adjustment ring. Dial indexes, hands, and the zero-mark on the rotating ring all have a luminescent coating.

The Sea Dweller case is waterproof to a depth of 3,000 feet (approximately 1,220m). Inside the patented case, which is worn on a so-called Fliplock bracelet with safety loop and fold-out extension, ticks an outstanding, specially crafted movement with official chronometer certificate, the Rolex Caliber 3135, automatically wound with a power reserve of fifty hours.

A Great Piece: Rolex Sea-Dweller Deep Sea

Year after year, piece by piece, Rolex updates its Oyster collection. After the Daytona, Submariner, and GMT-Master II, in 2008, came the Sea-Dweller with the suffix Deep Sea — the prototype of a hardcore diving watch. This new piece was introduced as follows:

"This watch is unforgettable. Once you've seen it, you know how a diving watch should look. Anyone who owns one will probably never leave it behind. Nearly a half-a-pound [a German pound = 1 pound/500g] less on the arm doesn't go unnoticed and, in the end, why should anyone take it off? Finally, Rolex has splashed out, giving the new Rolex Sea-Dweller Deep Sea, the very comfortable-to-wear metal bracelet that we have already praised on the GMT-Master II. However, since Rolex also pays attention to improvements in detail, the Deep Sea was given an even more improved clasp.

In the Rolex nomenclature, this answers to the name 'Glidelock,' which refers to a patented system that, thanks to fine increments, makes it possible to adjust the bracelet length by almost inch/millimeter-exact amounts. These adjustments make it also cling on a smaller wrist and, with the help of the so-called 'Fliplock' extension, even over a diving-suit up to 3/10" thick (7m)."

With this, the underwater sportsman could — purely theoretically — reach the wreck of the Titanic on the Atlantic Ocean floor. At least the Rolex would survive the dive un-damaged because it is pressure-tested at 390 bar, the equivalent of a diving depth of 12,795 feet (3,900m). To withstand such pressure, even the Oyster case had to get some modifications, despite being known to be very sturdy. Among the outwardly visible alterations are the 1/5" thick (5.5mm), slightly curved sapphire crystal and the slightly curved titanium back. Both crystal and back are supported by a forged stainless steel ring inte-grated into the case frame.

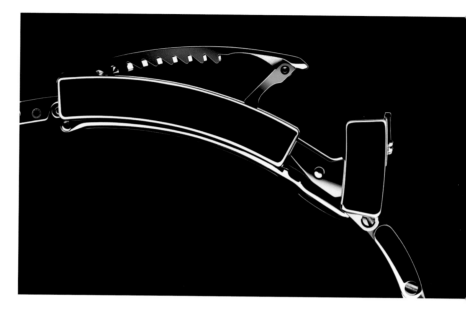

Sophisticated: The "Fliplock" watch band extension and the fine adjustment "Glide-lock" are integrated into the new clasp.

Rolex designers specifically borrowed this type of pressure load bal-ancing from building support structure architecture, specifically from church architecture, as a Rolex spokeswoman says. Rolex calls the interaction of back, crystal, and support ring, the "Ringlock system." Three seals ensure that no water penetrates, even through the tube of the screw-down crown. Each Deepsea has to undergo a water-proof test, which Rolex has developed together with the experts for Underwater Technology of COMEX (Compagnie Maritime d'Expertise) of France.

Readability is another improvement to the Sea-Dweller. The gold hands and index markers, compared to the previous ones, were en-larged and given a bright blue luminous coating, which is easier to see under water than white. This luminous material also adorns the

*Inconspicuous: The helium valve is
integrated discretely into the case.*

triangle on the dive ring, which the marks the zero point. The ring itself is covered with a ceramic layer in which the digits and interval marks are engraved and is platinum coated, using PVD technology.

Finally, the Deep Sea, as did its predecessor, has a helium valve that underlines its professional appearance. Professional divers pause in special capsules between two dives at great depths, where they breathe a high-pressure gas mixture that contains especially helium. During this time, helium diffuses, as a highly volatile gas, into the case. During the ascent, the pressure ratio alters and the helium influx can escape through the valve. Even ambitious diving amateurs won't need this feature, but sometimes it's just nice to know: You could, if you just wanted to.

Rolex also invested in the watch's intrinsic worth and improved the value of the already-sturdy automatic Caliber 3135 by using the high-quality Parachrom hairspring, which is insensitive to magnetic influences. The sum of technical improvements is also significantly reflected in the price. The Sea-Dweller Deep Sea can be had for 7,100 euros ($9,576 U.S. dollars).

"Double stitched": An additional steel ring reinforces the titanium back.

From Time to Time

When you are traveling, a watch that can be quickly set to the new local time without losing the home time is an advantage. The Rolex GMT-Master does this extremely well.

Typical of the GMT-Master II — as well as for many other Oyster models — is the magnifier integrated into the crystal, which enlarges the date display.

If someone takes a trip, he has, citing German poet Mathias Claudius, not only a lot to tell, but he must also keep different times in view: the local and home time. Ultimately, our earth is divided into twenty-four time zones, counted from the prime meridian and going east. This is due to the west-east direction rotation of the earth. The local time changes when traveling both in an easterly and westerly direction, and indeed — at least theoretically — it changes by one hour for every fifteen degrees longitude. Finally, the Earth turns once a day around its axis (360 degrees) and the day consists of twenty-four hours (360:24 = 15).

Great Britain laid the base for this reckoning by defining the prime meridian and, while the latitude zero, the Equator, is clearly defined geographically, the longitude zero was set arbitrarily. This was done by the Royal Observatory at Greenwich in London, in a Nautical Almanac, published in 1767. The English decided that the prime meridian, as the authoritative baseline for global time measurement, should run through the English capital — directly through the Observatory. This was confirmed by the international meridian conference in 1884, so that time reference was, from then on, known as "Greenwich Mean Time," or GMT. In international usage, today, we speak of "Coordi-

nated Universal Time" (CUT) instead of GMT. This is the time refer-ence for pilots or military personnel.

Germany today uses Central European Time (CET). This was intro-duced in 1893, with Paris as the reference location, and corresponds to Greenwich time plus one hour. For political and practical reasons, CET extends from the west coast of Spain to the eastern border of Poland, and thus covers a distance of nearly thirty-five degrees of longitude. This does not refute the initially described reckoning, but just qualifies it.

In 2007, Rolex introduced a fundamentally revised GMT-Master II. The scratch-resistant bezel with sapphire crystal is a substantial improvement.

At work in the GMT-Master II is Rolex's Caliber 3186 (base caliber 3135). It is distinguished by a 24-hour display, which always shows the home time. When traveling, you can independently set the hour-hand to the new time zone.

That shouldn't disturb us, however, and certainly not as watch connoisseurs. The time zone issue just gives us another good reason to occupy ourselves with a special kind of timepiece. In the event that we buy one, we not only get the sensation of a new ticker on the wrist, but the factual argument that this new companion is really useful and practical — at least, from time to time.

Rolex GMT-Master II: One for Everyone

It makes no difference if you're traveling by train, car, plane, or ship. Whether your trip requires a dark suit or a T-shirt and jeans is okay; whatever. With the Rolex GMT-Master II, you are always appropriately dressed — especially if your watch is in a simple stainless steel dress. Its appearance demonstrates the wearer's quality consciousness, particularly in the revised design.

The GMT-Master II made a good impression in comparisons with other watches with second time zones, including up against the much more expensive Vacheron Constantin Overseas Dual Time.

Its separately adjustable hour hand makes the GMT-Master II one of the most functional mechanical travel watches.

The House of Rolex's conservative model policy has left much as always, and the only alterations made to the watch were necessary ones. The result is many improvements in detail. These included the current scratch-resistant and UV-resistant ceramic bezel. The engraved numerals and index markers are platinum encrusted, so that even someone buying a steel watch can enjoy some precious metal. The bilaterally rotatable bezel maintains a clean hourly rhythm. By the way, dear collectors, the days of two-color bezels (e.g., blue/red) are over.

Instead of the double sealed "Twinlock" crown previously installed in this watch, the designers of the GMT-Master have now splashed out on an additionally sealed "Triplock" crown, also used in the diver's watches, the "Submariner" and "Sea-Dweller." The specified waterproof quality stays at 10 atm. For the bracelet, Rolex made what is, in the truest sense of the word, a tangible quality leap. If the predecessor model's bracelet was what evil tongues called "rickety," the new "Oysterlock" bracelet is above criticism. There is no longer any play in the joints of the bracelet links and the folding clasp is milled from a solid piece, not, as before, made of formed sheet steel; it now closes and opens comfortably. The integrated, approximately 1/5" (5mm) extension is a very useful detail: this helps the bracelet conform to the wearer's different arm circumferences in the summer and winter.

Something has also been done about the watch's inner life. Although this is still based on the standard Rolex automatic movement Caliber 3135, it is no longer designated 3185, but 3186. The essential difference lies in the regulator or, more precisely, the spiral spring. Rolex has installed the blue Parachrom hairspring, which they develop and produce itself. According to Rolex, the alloy used to make this spring completely non-magnetic and significantly more shock-resistant than that used in other commercially available hairsprings. Like all Rolex watches, the GMT-Master II is also chronometer-tested.

In a Rolex, the GMT function is always controlled by the crown, thus making it a role model for many other manufacturers. At the first lock-in position, the hour-hand can be separately set forward or back, without stopping the watch in the process. When it moves over the 24-hour marker, the date also jumps. The home time is shown by a traditional 24-hour hand with a large arrowhead. This is no longer made bright red, but kept in the House's subtle dark green color. So… have a good trip.

Precious? Steel! – The Rolex GMT-Master

In the January 1997 issue of the German magazine ArmbandUhren (Wristwatches), the editors compared nine luxury steel watches. A GMT-Master, representing this exalted test field, adorned the cover. With its characteristic blue-red rotating bezel, it is an eye-catcher. The editors were also aware that: "Anyone who doesn't recognize a Rolex GMT-Master, already at a hundred paces, needs glasses — or has lived on the other side of the Moon for the last few years." Here, this character actor from Geneva is in a comparison review with the most prominent cast possible, including the Blancpain 2100, the Nautilus by Patek Philippe, the Vacheron Constantin Overseas, and the Audemars Piguet Royal Oak.

However, the editors did not provide any clear recommendations for making a purchase, as they explained: "This was no watch test, so there was no defined winner or loser in this comparison of sporty luxury steel watches. The extremely broad price differences, from $3,000 to $19,000 (U.S. dollars today), alone already prohibit applying any rigid rating scale for individual criterion, and if a (subjectively) easily-workable clasp could compensate for a (subjectively) hard-to-read dial, surely that should be up to any watch buyer's personal

Rolex Oyster Perpetual GMT-Master II

Reference No.: 116710LN
Movement: Rolex Caliber 3186, Base Rolex 3135, diameter 1-1/10" (28.5mm), height 1/4" (6.4mm), 31 jewels; 28,800-vph, automatic; stop seconds device; power reserve 48 hours; tested chronometer (COSC)
Functions: Hours, minutes, seconds, date; separately adjustable hour-hand, analog 24-hour display (second time zone)
Case: Stainless steel, polished/matt, sapphire crystal, screw-down steel back; screw-down "Triplock" crown; pressure resistant up to 10 atm, diameter 1-3/5" (40mm), height ½" (12.1mm)
Weight: 5-1/2 ounces (155g)
Bracelet: "Oysterlock" steel bracelet with folding clasp and integrated extension
Price: When introduced, 5,350 euro ($7,385 U.S. dollars)
Options: Steel/yellow gold ("Rolesor"), 7,780 euros ($10,740 U.S. dollars)

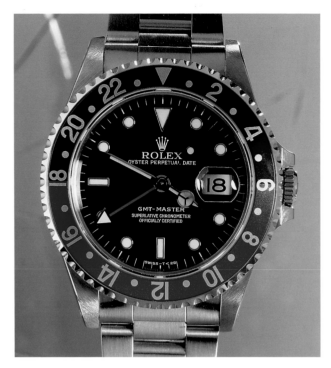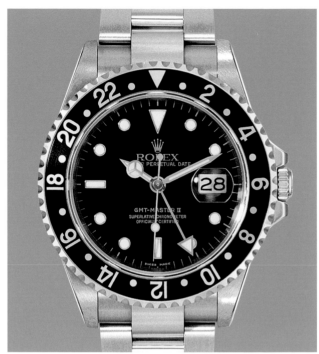

The vintage steel GMT has the blue-red bezel beloved of buyers (left). For the steel-gold version, Rolex went for a golden 24-hour hand (right).

preferences. Watches, especially expensive mechanical watches, must be pleasing in the first place. In the end, it was the — debatable — specific features of a particular model, which led in some cases to rejection or enthusiasm; this is why for such watches any per se standardized consideration or 'comparison test' just doesn't work in the long-term."

However, none of this prevented the editors from evaluating the candidates with a critical eye. The Master GMT's movement earned unqualified praise: "We like to compare it with a tractor (though with four-wheel drive, ABS, and air-conditioned cabin): the Rolex GMT Master Caliber 3175, derived from the base Caliber 3135 (just with date), with an additional central 24-hour hand. The finish is flawless, despite large-scale production, as is the performance of the officially-tested chronometer movement. From the 1/5" (6mm) design height, you can not only conclude the vintage, mature construction, but also the sturdy dimensions of the drive components."

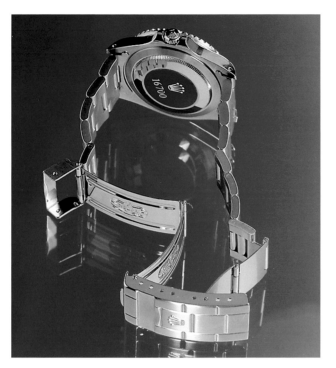

The bracelet and clasp of the older GMT models often gave fans and journalists cause for criticism (left); however, the Caliber 3175 has always been held up as a reference point.

The shell in which this movement works also gets broad recognition — as in the other test candidates: "The case creates a very positive impression throughout in terms of workmanship and processing." The Rolex steel bracelet, however, is a point of criticism: "Tiny folded bands such as Rolex's 'Oyster Fliplock,' are a relic from the 1970s, and the, in principle, model (and often-enough imitated) clasp technology with folding safety catch against accidental opening, isn't ... convincing."

Nevertheless, the editors considered the GMT-Master — as well as the other competitors — a good buy: "They are through and through sturdy structures, have a distinctive, heavy, and rock-solid steel case with scratch-resistant sapphire crystal and could take a small poke. An (intentional or unintentional) water bath can't harm them at all, and the solid steel link bracelets forge them to your wrist, so they can't be lost. However, they differ from the majority of commercially available sports watches, through a mysterious, distinguished, luxurious radiance, which itself (throughout quite different parts) comes from the knowledge of the watches' origin and inner workings, design finesse, and qualitatively very high-quality workmanship."

Rolex GMT Master

Reference No.: 16700
Functions: Hours, minutes, seconds, date, 24 hours
Movement: Rolex Caliber 3175, 28,800vph, diameter 1-1/10" (28.5mm), height 1/5" (6mm), officially-certified chronometer
Dial: Applied, mounted, round and wedge luminous coated index markers, luminous triangles
Case: Stainless steel, diameter 1-1/2" (40mm), height 1/2" (12mm)
Bracelet: Stainless steel, simple, diving safety catch ("Fliplock")
Weight: 4-1/5 ounces (120g)
Price: When introduced, 4,800 DM (approx. € 2,400) [$6,477/$3,238.50 U.S. dollars]

Long Live Sports

Not Just for the Short Term

Rolex chronographs embody the prototype of a prestigious sports timepiece; in the world of successful men, they enjoy almost the status of an exotic sports car. However, where does the watch end and the myth begin? Some answers to these questions were found in the history and technology of the new Daytona watch model, which was introduced in 2000.

The Rolex Daytona "Paul Newman": It wrote a piece of watch history and stirred up the watch market.

For most inhabitants of the civilized world, a Rolex is synonymous with the commercial and social success of its wearer; at the same time, it is a product that advertises itself. As a result, Rolex is one of the best-known watch brands in the world. Today, chronographs of the highest quality play an essential role in this development.

The second edition of this Rolex success model already had a screw-down pusher.

While chronographs with the Rolex label already existed in the 1920s, '30s, and '40s, their rather restrained charisma can't compare with the fascination that the newer successors wield on their public. These modern Rolex chronographs are called "Daytona," named after the popular tourist town Daytona, Florida, only a few miles away from Miami and the NASA space center at Cape Canaveral.

Two historic Rolex chronographs from the 1920s and '30s.

This place name has a special ring in the ears of automobile enthusiasts because one of the most famous motor races in the world has taken place on the same-named racetrack since the 1960s: the Rolex 24 Hours at Daytona. It was obvious that Rolex would use this prestigious name, especially since the 1961 model "Oyster Cosmograph" (Ref. 6239) had opened a new dimension of sportsmanship that practically forced comparison with the fascinating world of auto-racing.

However, the first Daytona chronograph (officially still called a "cosmograph"), in a screw-down Oyster case — first in steel, later in 14-carat (for the European market, 18-carat) gold — with waterproof screw-down crown and round pushers, did not achieve overwhelming success, at least not by today's standards. This could likely be primarily traced back to the base watch movement of the Caliber Valjoux 72, with a manual-winding mechanism that was something of an anachronism in the era of automatic watches.

Rectangular chronometers were very popular in the 1940s.

In addition to a version with dark dial (Ref. 6241), there was also a version unofficially carrying the extra label "Paul Newman," which had additional scales and minute-display in contrasting colors (brown and beige for gold models; white and brown for the steel version). We trace this name back to a movie made with the breathtaking backdrop of the "Carrera Panamericana" automobile endurance race, where the actor conspicuously wore a Daytona model especially developed for the American market model on his wrist; this model, in contrast to those intended for European customers, always had a small red "Daytona" logo above the 12-hour counter by the 6.

83

Above, a "Daytona" cosmograph; right and below, two recent models with 400 tachymeter scale.

In 1976, with the introduction of a screw-down push piece, the cosmograph got its first upgrade. There was a series (Ref. 6263) with black bezel and one (Ref. 6265) with engraved and polished bezel. However, it would take until 1988 before the "Oyster cosmograph" became the "Oyster Perpetual cosmograph" and, as the name indicates, got an automatic-winding mechanism. In a newly developed case, there was now ticking a new movement, which — while not developed completely in-house — still demonstrated a high degree of autonomy. As the base movement, Rolex installed the integrated Zenith chronograph Caliber 400; with immense input, this was modified in more than two hundred details. The most drastic change in the legendary "El Primero" Caliber 400 entailed reducing the cadence from 36,000 to 28,800 vibrations per hour by mounting its own balance. Rolex also waived the date-window display at the 4. The first series of automatic Daytonas got a tachymeter bezel reaching up to 200 "units per hour," which, in the era of the 300 km-per-hour super sports' cars, would be like expanding the stroke of a Ferrari F40 up to 400.

Although the Daytona, unlike the above-mentioned Ferrari, was not conceived of as a "limited edition," the resale prices of both products developed in a surprisingly similar way at the end of the 1980s. Shortly after they were introduced, you could only get both the Ferrari and the Rolex from the factory after a considerable delivery time; this of course, sent the prices of the pieces available rapidly skyrocketing. In anticipation of good profits, Rolex was smart enough not to let production of the Daytona rise excessively, but always kept the market tight with constant production figures.

The Millennium Movement: Rolex's Own Chronograph Caliber

The second chronograph sensation of 2000 came with the news, first leaked just a few days before the Basel Fair opened, that Rolex would finally equip the Chrono success "Daytona" with its own watch movement. This meant that Rolex concessionaires got some pretty uncomfortable questions from customers over the next several months, including: "Does this watch have a new movement inside or still the old one?" In collectors' circles, the assessment of which of the two movements is the better one, has not yet been cleared up even today.

From the beginning, however, it was clear that the new watch movement was more in demand with non-collectors, but those customers should be wary of undervaluing the broadly-modified Zenith chronograph movement used up to now. In closer comparison, it would not be so easy for the Rolex Caliber 4130 to surpass the established "Primero," at least in terms of finish and design aesthetics — but on these issues, the Rolex design engineers have always had their own views.

Rolex Daytona Cosmograph Ref. 116519 in 18-carat white gold, with crocodile leather strap and folding clasp. This model has an understated elegance, in which the harmony between the black dial and matching-colored leather strap plays a role. The connoisseur will know from the matte gleam of the case that here we have a noble precious metal and no steel alloy. The Rolex Daytona cosmograph was already launched in 2000, but today is still in top place in many watch enthusiasts' wish lists. The solid screw-down back gives "bomb-proof" protection and cover to the chronograph movement 4130.

The new movement has certainly become rugged, and has already sufficiently demonstrated the proverbial reliability of a tractor when put to the test (perhaps here one should better speak of being tied to a "martyr's stake"). From a design point of view, the indestructible qualities of the Caliber 4130 speak to positioning the quite large balance (with the Rolex-invented "Microstella" adjustable screws) on a stable bridge instead of a protruding, cantilevered clock. Through decentralized mounting of the chronograph's lever mechanism, with classic intermediate wheel control, on the rear plate, it was possible to keep the watch movement height limited to 1/4" (6.5mm), despite the winding mechanism oscillating weight rotating in a ball bearing. Increased value was put on a particularly high power reserve: When fully wound, the Daytona movement runs for seventy-two hours in the "green area," i.e. at chronometer standard. That should suffice when you take the watch off for the weekend and put it back on your wrist on Monday without any annoying winding and setting — the "cosmograph" is ultimately an everyday watch and no chic dinner party accessory. Anyway, this is how they see things at Rolex, even if they had not thought to correct the imbalance in distribution of production numbers between steel and gold cases … evil to him who thinks evil.

However, author Peter Brown, of the U.K., was not so completely in agreement with the argumentation ("unconditional reliability and practicality") of Rolex chief for Germany Peter Streit because to round out the image of such an expensive watch (the new cosmograph is about 7% more expensive than the old one), there must also be a certain degree of what the English so un-translatably call "sophistication" — a similar quality assessment of luxury cars these days. It is exactly this that the author found somewhat wanting in the new Rolex chronograph: "If a comparison with a Mercedes in the past appeared somewhat overdone, yet the image of the Range Rover works quite well: this high-class, British off-road vehicle shows, even in extreme terrain, similar staying qualities to the 'cosmograph,' which is very sporty, as the reason its his being; yet its occupants don't have to do without the comforts of air-conditioning and electric seat heating. From this (car) perspective, the Daytona looks perhaps more like a 'Hummer'." This view, from 2000, is today, in part, refuted. While the "Hummer" brand is on the brink of extinction, the Rolex Daytona enjoys a steady popularity.

The Bottom Line: The In-House Workshop Quality Movement Makes the Difference

The quintessence, or bottom line, means a category in which five comparable watches are taken under consideration, but without any evaluation on a point system. In the fall of 2007, five manufacturer's in-house chronographs made their appearance: the Rolex Daytona took on the Breguet Marine Chronograph, the Chopard LUC Chrono One, the IWC Da Vinci, and the Zenith Chronomaster XL:

The watch industry also uses evocative names of distant cities and countries to try to promote sales of their products; by just reading watch catalogs, you can take an imaginary round-the-world trip. "Marrakesh," "Hampton," "Casablanca," "Melbourne," "Panama," "Porto Rotondo" — there are countless examples of wristwatches that are promoted, with aid of some Wanderlust, to lure consumers with thoughts of exotic holiday destinations into the local jewelry store.

Rolex Caliber 4130 in Rolex movement holder Ref. 2240.

1.) Rotor and balance bridge define the first impression. In contrast to the other Rolex automatic movements, the rotor axle seating is not set in two ruby bearings, but runs on a ball bearing.

2.) After removing the rotor, you see the structure of the design: the automatic bridge is positioned above right, recognizable by the red and yellow anodized aluminum gear wheels. The caliber number, 4130, is engraved in the adjacent bridge for the chronograph.

3.) In this picture, the automatic bridge is dismantled. Below is the stable balance bridge with balance. Thanks to Breguet overcoil springs and the four "Microstella" adjustable screws, this movement can be regulated very exactly.

4.) After the bridge for the chronograph was removed, we can see, below left, the almost V-shaped hammer or heart lever. At its right end, you can recognize the hour; at the left end, the minute counter wheel. Between is the elaborate vertical coupling, with a gear wheel that intermeshes with the second wheel for the chronograph.

5.) After the chronometer components are removed, the Y-shaped train wheel bridge can be seen. At left, you can see the intermediate wheel; at the top, the crown and ratchet wheels.

6.) Finally, the base plate with oscillation system, train wheels, and barrel. By them, are positioned the center, third, and second wheels. ert.

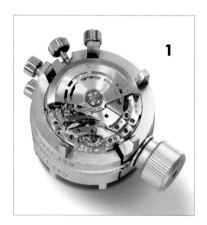

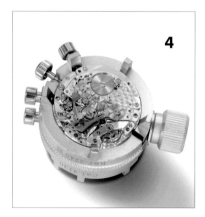

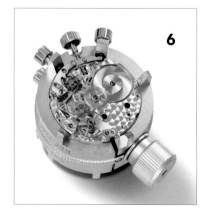

Like the watch hands, the small boat/shuttle-shaped hour index markers are made of gold and are coated with the luminescent material "Super Luminova."

"Daytona," more exactly Daytona Beach, is such a well-sounding name—one of those beach resorts scattered like pearls along Florida's east coast—but with this name, it is mainly motor-racing fans who sit up and take note. It is here that an annual, well-endowed "24 Hour Race" is held, which has sometimes even been honored by Hollywood. Rolex, therefore, once named a sports chronograph "Daytona" and immediately bestowed one on the then-young actor Paul Newman.

A Rolex, which is many a watch lover's dream, is also equipped with a chronograph and is almost a "must" for the sports watch enthusiast; with the addition of this name that inspires the imagination, there is no doubt that the "Cosmograph Rolex Daytona" had all the ingredients for a fantastic success, and then, when the cult-status Rolex Daytona watch, due to strong demand and limited production capacity in the 1990s, also became "limited" — it was only available after a waiting period of up to two years — this drove the watch market totally crazy. Shrewd businessmen could demand black market prices up to twice the original price for a Rolex Daytona, and these amounts were also paid by watch enthusiasts who were as fanatical as they were well-heeled.

As a result of almost seven years of development, manufacturing, and testing work, in 2000, Rolex introduced its first Daytona with its own chronograph movement. The Caliber 4130 is equipped with a balance bridge for stability and further adjusting balance end-shake. In this movement, the oscillating system itself is also adjusted without

The "Rolésor" case (Rolex's name for this stainless steel-gold compound) is 1/2" high (12.8mm) and has the typical screw-down back with precision interlock, with a hologram label to protect against counterfeiting. Pushers and crown can be screwed down.

index pin and regulator. While other top watch brands only first introduced adjustment systems recently, so that the balance wheel can "breathe" freely (which is only partially possible with traditional devices), the Geneva luxury brand has been using the "Microstella" system for many years. In this system, tiny, star-shaped nuts are screwed onto the threaded socket on the inner side of the balance rim. Using a special key, which has a scale and movable gauge segment on its handle, the star-shaped nuts can be rotated outwards or inwards to allow adjustment of the balance inertia. The watchmaker can read rate alterations in seconds on the scale.

The Caliber 4130 has a diameter of 1-1/5" (30mm) and runs for seventy-two hours when fully wound. The Rolex chronograph presented has a "Rolésor" case, which has a crystal rim of 18-carat gold on its stainless steel shell and is also equipped with gold pushers and winding crown. The watch's hour index markers and hands are also made of the precious metal, here alloyed with copper, to obtain the reddish hue. The stable link bracelet and folding clasp in stainless steel also have a middle strip of gold. The bezel has an engraved, black-encrusted counter scale, provided primarily for calculating speed with the chronograph.

The sturdy folding clasp, which Rolex named the "Oysterclasp," is also in made in stainless steel/gold.

Technology: The Rolex Chronograph Movement

In a "somewhat different watch test," the editors of ArmbandUhren /"Wristwatches" put the technology of four in-house chronographs under the microscope. Among them, of course, was the Rolex Daytona, with the in-house Caliber 4130 — in fact, in triplicate. Because the test team had selected the Rolex Daytona as a reference, in addition to the test watch provided by Rolex, two more Daytonas were anonymously purchased from concessionaires. This created a statistically reliable basis, to prevent any possible under- or over-valuation of the Rolex brand.

To determine accuracy, the watches were both measured under laboratory conditions on an electronic timescale (Chronoscope S1 with Mikromat S) and also subjected to a practical wearing test. In this, the tester determined the daily performance each morning and evening,

The Caliber 4130, introduced in 2000, is equipped with a balance bridge for stability and further adjusting balance end-shake. It has a diameter of 1-1/5" (30mm) and runs seventy-two hours when fully wound.

over fourteen days, and the result was logged on a form. The rate deviation was determined by radio clock or telephone time.

The practical testing of the white gold Daytona was undertaken by editor-in-chief Peter Braun. His assessment was that the chronograph is comfortably dimensioned, and, in his opinion, sat well on his left wrist. Only the safety catch on the folding clasp opened occasionally. The performance was described as excellent. Braun judged the appearance as positive throughout; it did not have the otherwise well-known "Rolex factor." The review of the two anonymously purchased Rolex Daytona watches was undertaken by two ambitious watch enthusiasts (and readers of the magazine): Peter Reiser from Cologne, Germany, and Ingolf Menius from Stuttgart, Germany. Both gave their Daytona highest marks for practical value and overall impression. Comfort and appearance also received high praise.

For accuracy, the grade was excellent. The white gold Rolex was perfectly adjusted from the factory. On the timer, there was a daily gain of two seconds, which is already fully within chronometer standards. In the two-week field trial, the watch fulfilled the test almost without any rate deviation. The two purchased Daytona models conducted themselves just as valiantly. They completed the laboratory tests with plus 0.6 seconds/day and plus 1.3 seconds per day. In practice, they went just three and seven seconds ahead after two weeks, and were, of course, not corrected manually during this time. These outstanding results confirm, in the opinion of the reviewer, the entirely positive impression that the design of the watch movement had already delivered: "With the clean technical solution on the one hand and the small number of a total of 201 single parts on the other, you have, in fact, achieved excellent results in this Caliber. It may, therefore, not only be cited as a reference for the other chronograph movements, but also in general, as a role model."

Rolex Cosmograph Daytona

Reference No.: 11 65 23
Movement: Rolex Caliber 4130, diameter 1-1/5" (30mm), height 1/5" (4.6mm), 44 jewels; automatic, 28,800vph, power reserve 22 hours, stop second
Functions: Hour, minute, small second-hand, date, chronograph with second, 30-minute and 12-hour counters
Dial: Silver-plated; black printed minute track; applied, faceted, and polished golden luminescent hour index markers; faceted luminescent gold hands
Case: Diameter 1-3/5" (40mm), height 1/2" (12.8mm), stainless steel, polished; red-gold bezel, 750/000; sapphire crystal; polished stainless steel back, fully threaded; screw-down pushers and crown; waterproof to 328 feet (100m).
Bracelet: "Oysterlock" stainless steel-gold link bracelet; "Oyster-clasp" stainless steel-gold folding clasp, safety catch with brand emblem.
Special Feature: Vertical chronograph clutch; chronometer certificate
Price: When introduced,10,190 euros ($13,772 U.S. dollars today)

Rolex Regatta

The Yacht-Master would have fit in among the "tool watch-es" in the previous chapter. Originally, it was no more than a very accurate automatic watch with date display and rotating bezel. Since 2007, it has been called the Rolex Oyster Perpetual Yacht-Master II and is a chronograph, even if that is not apparent at first glance. This is why the timer, with its minute-interval programmable countdown counter, was chosen as the "grown man's toy of the year."

The Yacht-Master II's rotatable bezel is called "Ring Command." It controls the count-down timer.

With its almost 1-7/10" (43mm) diameter, the Yacht-Master II is the largest of
all current Rolex models and, literally,
its flagship. The red arrow points to the
set countdown time.

The new Yacht-Master II may not be the first mechanical wristwatch with a programmable countdown function, but it is the first such watch, with its impeccable waterproof qualities, that you would want to take aboard a racing yacht.

The Yacht-Master II is equipped with the new Caliber 4160; its 360 components give watch connoisseurs an idea just how complex this mechanism is. Like the Daytona chronograph movement Caliber 4130, to which it is related, the 4160 has an intermediate wheel and vertical clutch. The heart of the movement beats at 28,800-vph and is equipped with a blue Parachrom Breguet spring by Rolex, which is over ten times more shock resistant and less sensitive to magnetic fields. Of course, the movement was tested for accuracy by the independent Swiss testing authority COSC (Contrôle Officiel Suisse des Chronomèter).

The countdown timer can be pre-programmed in minute increments (up to a maximum of ten minutes) and is operated via two pushers and the unidirectional 90° rotating "Ring Command" bezel. The settings can be made on the watch with one hand, but, to do this, you first have to understand the system.

No, it's not steel. The white gold Yacht-Master II with platinum bezel makes its visual impact with discreet understatement.

Turning the "Ring Command" bezel blocks the start-stop pusher (by the "2") while simultaneously enabling an additional crown function. Now, if you push the reset button (by the "4") and engage it, the winding crown will, in position 1 (normally "wind up"), directly operate the countdown minute hand. This can be set to the countdown time in one-minute intervals. When you turn the bezel back to its original position, the reset button jumps back out and the crown can be screwed watertight.

Pressing the (now again unlatched) start-stop push button initiates the countdown measurement. Of course, it can be interrupted at any time by re-pressing the start-stop pusher and also re-started. When the measurement stops, pressure on the reset button will set the countdown to the last pre-set time. The highlight: When the measurement is running, the reset functions like a flyback, i.e., the second hand jumps back to zero and the minute counter to the previous, or next, minute depending on the setting of the second hand. This means, you can synchronize an already started countdown to an official visual or sound signal.

The Yacht-Master II case has a diameter of 1-7/10" (42.6mm) and is made from a solid block of yellow or white gold. The bezel of the yellow gold version (about 24,000 euro/$32,441 U.S. dollars), features a blue ceramic numeral plate that maybe a bit too much even bears the lettering "Yacht-Master II." The bezel of the white gold version (about 28,000 euro/$37,842 U.S. dollars), however, is made of platinum and displays the numerals in relief.

This Sports Fan Is a Stickler for Accuracy

Despite the initial impression, this vintage Yacht-Master is no diving watch.

In its March 2006 issue, the editors of the German magazine ArmbandUhren (Wristwatches) offered a comprehensive dossier on the subject "chronometer." It also included a "bottom line" comprising five chronometers of differing provenance and price range. Rolex can't fail to be there; basically, the House is the chief customer of the official testing institute COSC. Already, in 2004, the lion's share of the chronometer certificates were issued to Rolex, which had no fewer than 628,556 watch movements successfully tested by the COSC; the COSC had tested about 1.05 million watch movements during 2004. Every one of the sporty, elegant watches of the big Oyster model family is equipped with a watch movement that has passed the approximately two-week test.

The movement Caliber 3135 has been manufactured for almost twenty years (debut in 1988) and received numerous chronometer certificates.

The "Oyster Perpetual Date Yacht-Master" of 2006, an automatic sports watch with date display and rotating bezel, is an eloquent example of how it is possible to create a new model by making minor modifications. Ultimately, the Yacht-Master is very closely related to the Submariner, but is not a true diving watch because the adjustment ring with its classic diver's markings can be turned in both directions. Utilization of the same chronometer movement emphasizes all the more the relationship between Submariner and Yacht-Master.

This Caliber, 3135, was already designed in 1988, but many details have been altered since then to conform to state-of-the-art technology. The seating of the upper (facing the case back) balance pivot is characteristic of the in-house watch movement. Normally, the shock absorber, with a hole and cap jewel, sits in a cock, which only rests on one side of the base plate. The Caliber 3135 uses a balance bridge. Another feature: The bridge rests on two knurled nuts that can be rotated on the two movement pillars. This design makes it possible to alter the "mountain air," the axial play of the balance staff, even for already assembled watch movements, without changing the angle of the balance bearing to the balance staff.

To protect against scratching, but also to make life a little harder for counterfeiters, the Rolex case back comes with a sticker showing a printed serial number, made of special material that has a particular texture.

Rolex's "Oyster Perpetual Date Yacht-Master" has a stainless steel case with platinum rotating bezel. Characteristic are the especially large hour markers on this watch; they are set on a solid platinum dial—and the "Cyclops" magnifier over the date display.

The Yacht-Master has a 1/2" (12mm) high case.

In keeping with the understatement for which Rolex is known, the Yacht-Master dial is not only made of solid platinum, but the bezel also, which is set on a case milled from a stainless steel block using some 160 work steps. Rolex calls this compound "Rolesium"; the name combines the last letters of the English word "platinum" with the Geneva-based brand's own name. The matt platinum bezel, set on four ball bearings, is not only very easy to turn, but also stops exactly. It also has relief-form, high-gloss numerals and minute-interval markers milled from a solid block.

The anthracite gray dial with its unmistakable imprint, "Superlative Chronometer," where the broad, luminescent coated (Super-LumiNova) hands gently turn, bears extra large hour-interval markers. The model name, printed in bright red on the dial, and same-color second hand, give the otherwise subtle gray-silver mix that is distinctive to this watch — a welcome, almost sassy, color scheme.

Rolex Yacht-Master Rolesium

Reference No.: 78760-20
Movement: Rolex Caliber 3135; diameter 1" (25.5mm), height 1/5" (5.05mm); 25 jewels, automatic; 28,800-vph; power reserve 44 hours; stop-second
Case: Diameter 1-1/2" (40mm); height ½" (12mm); stainless steel, polished and matt; sapphire crystal with integrated date magnifier; platinum adjustment ring; stainless steel fully threaded screw-down back; waterproof to 328 feet (100m)
Dial: Platinum, gray painted, printed black minute track; luminescent applied hour interval markers; polished white gold hands
Bracelet: Stainless steel link bracelet; folding clasp with safety catch; brand logo and emblem
Special Features: Officially certified chronometer with COSC certificate; screw-down crown
Price: When introduced, 6,670 euros ($9,000 U.S. dollars today)

Dignified
Elegance

Something for Everyone

It goes just as well with an elegant three-piece suit as with jeans and appears distinctive without being pretentious, but, above all, this is a very good mechanical watch that fulfills the wish to get an in-house made, workshop-quality product at a reasonable price. As a result, the Rolex Datejust, even if it has been manufactured from 1945 to 2006 with only minimal alterations, is always a recurring theme.

An "Oyster Perpetual Datejust Chronometer" from 1952—the chronometer accuracy was tested at the Biel Observatory.

"In-house"-manufactured is a magic term, as much among watch lovers as among watchmakers. Today, this term encompasses the best possible representation of particularly high quality standards and correspondingly high prices, but what is actually behind the somewhat vague concept represented by the German word "Manufaktur" [in-house workshop crafted quality]? The consensus is likely that substantial parts of a watch movement must be manufactured in the brand's own production facilities and workshops, if the maker wants to adorn itself with that lucrative attribute "Manufaktur" [in-house made]. In today's understanding, the capacity to produce blank movements and essential movement parts in-house makes a watch factory into a workshop.

Watch enthusiasts must certainly say goodbye to the idea that in-house, manufactured products are completely hand-crafted. After all, it is the automatic lathes and modern computer-controlled machine tools that can manufacture watch movement parts with a precision that handwork, especially when making large numbers of pieces, could not attain.

Rolex "Oyster Perpetual Datejust Turn-O-Graph": Steel case with bilateral rotatable bezel in white gold 750/000, diameter 1-2/5" (36.4mm); sapphire crystal with inset date magnifier; steel back with full threading; steel link bracelet with folding clasp; automatic movement. Price: EUR 4,040/$5,454 U.S.

The movement: Rolex Caliber 3135, diameter 1-1/10" (28.5mm), height 1/5" (6mm); 31 jewels; automatic; 28,800-vph; power reserve 48 hours; COSC-certified chronometer.

However, the decorations of the movement components, such as the high-gloss (so-called "black") polishing of the heads of screws barely visible to the naked eye or the beveled edges of the cocks and movement bridges, beautified with a sophisticated pressure polishing, are the results of, what is in part, painstaking handwork. Especially when the movements are being assembled, an experienced expert's hand is still always in demand. Although they are insignificant for the way the watch movement actually functions, these so-called "finishing" steps are what make the difference between a "first class" and a "luxury movement." It is out of the combination of these engineering achievements, precision micro-machine engineering, use of high-quality materials, watch-making artistry, and perfect design of the watch movement, case, dial, and hands, that, in the end, manufacture-quality, workshop-crafted watches come into being.

If you apply all the above criteria as a yardstick, Rolex is a workshop in the best sense, yet at the same time counts within the Swiss watch industry as the brand with the largest self-reliance and most comprehensive manufacturing capabilities. First, the movements are produced almost entirely in-house; second, Rolex also produces its own cases.

In case design, the traditional Geneva House shows itself, obviously for good reason, to be very conservative. Most watches are installed in the same "Oyster" case that has proven its worth over decades and which has gotten only the occasional update with minor changes, depending on the model. Thus, the case design for an elegant watch like the Datejust and the sporty Submariner are basically the same. The Datejust lacks only side protectors for the winding crown and diving bezel. One Datejust style, the "Oyster Perpetual Datejust Turn-O-Graph," at least has a bidirectional rotating bezel, letting it fill in for outsiders the barely perceivable gap in the collection between pure sports and dress watches.

According to Rolex nomenclature, the movement ticking in the "Oyster Perpetual Datejust Turn-O-Graph" is an automatic that still only displays the date along with the time. This is the House of Rolex's most-produced Caliber, 3135, which has been discussed earlier in this book. As a result, discussion here will be limited to the chronometer-certified, manufactured-caliber essentials.

For watch movements, Rolex has pursued paths different from those taken by other manufacturers, and the majority of movements manage without conventional regulating mechanisms. While other manufacturers reactivated the swan's neck fine adjustment system, for a long time Rolex has done without index pins, regulators, and regulator pointers, which, as is well-known, are moved by this very regulating mechanism. Regulation is done directly by the balance, in that the tiny, star-shaped nuts set on delicate thread "bolts" on the balance rim can be adjusted with a special tool to alter the center of gravity of the balance weight and, with this, the actual rate. The balance itself oscillates under a double-sided bridge lying on the base plate (in contrast to a balance cock fixed on one side), which creates optimal stability for the balance bearings.

This Rolex is 1/2" high (12.3mm).

The bracelet's satinized folding clasp bears the trademark symbol.

Rolex covers the screw-down back with a protective film showing a kind of hologram.

107

Rolex Oyster Perpetual Datejust Turn-O-Graph

Reference No.: 16264
Movement: Rolex Caliber 3135; automatic; diameter 1-1/10" (28.5mm), height 1/5" (6mm); 31 jewels, 28.800-vph; power reserve 48 hours; certified chronometer
Features: Hours, minutes, central second hand; date
Dial: Lacquered white; black imprinted minute track (chemin de fer [railway]); applied, polished hour index markers and Rolex crown at the "12"; polished luminescent coated steel hands
Case: Diameter 1-2/5" (36.4mm), height 1/2" (12.3mm); steel, polished and matt; sapphire crystal with integrated date magnifier; polished and matt fully threaded steel screw-down back; waterproof to 328 feet (100m)
Bracelet: Steel link bracelet; steel folding clasp with brand logo
Special features: Bilateral rotating bezel in white gold; screw-down crown
Price: When introduced, 4,040 euros ($5,454 U.S.)

The seating of the Caliber 3135's automatic oscillating weight is also unusual. There is no fixed axle; rather, the rotor shaft is set in the jewel bearing from above and held from below, under the automatic bridge, by a small forked lever or pallet that spring-catches in a groove in the shaft. The index wheels of the automatic winding mechanism are attention-getters with their eye-catching purple color. This is caused by a coating to harden the surface of the brass wheels, which lets them work basically maintenance-free.

Always Up-To-Date

Rolex, and hence the Datejust, is not exclusively a male thing. After all, this model is currently available in various sizes and gladly refined with precious metals and diamonds. In its 2006 pre-Christmas edition, the German magazine ArmbandUhren/"Wristwatches" showed, under the headline "Hours of togetherness," a couple offering the perfect partner look: A Datejust with 1-2/5" (37mm) case, initially man-oriented, but often happily worn by ladies. Joining them is the definitely just-for-the-ladies model, in the very traditional women's size with only 1" (26mm) diameter.

The hidden folding clasp with newly refined opening mechanism adorns the 1" (26mm) diameter ladies' model.

A Datejust can be subtle, but doesn't have to be. This lavishly be-diamonded version is more suitable as evening jew- elry than as an everyday watch.

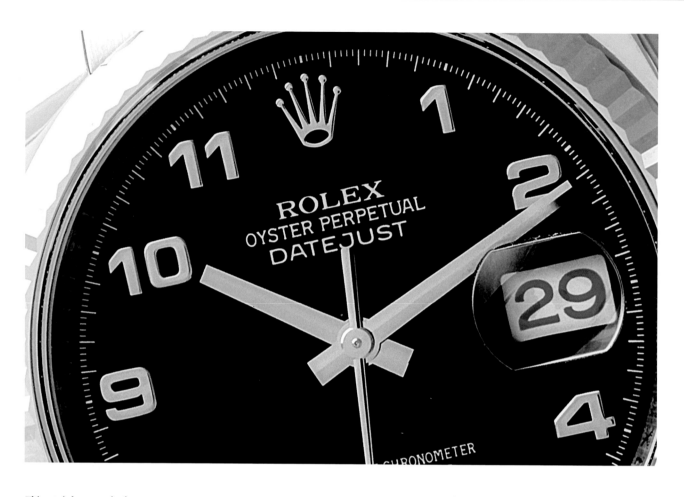

This stainless steel chronometer combines a white gold bezel, with self-winding proprietary movement of course chronometer standard (COSC) certified with Arabic numerals on black background; it is worn on a solid Oyster bracelet with satinized outside links and polished inner links (4,465 euros/$6,025 U.S. dollars).

While the 1-2/5" (37mm) model with plain Arabic numerals makes a very discreet impression, the Lady Datejust is indeed very feminine and gleams with diamond hour-index markers on the dial. Another extravagance on both watches, which can't be recognized at first sight, and increases the understatement: both steel watches have bezels made of white gold, also known in Rolex parlance as "white Rolésor."

The case conforms to the new Datejust generation, which was introduced at the 2006 BaselWorld international conference. In the author's view, the remolding of this Rolex classic is almost a revolution in itself. That may sound extreme, but the notion of facelift or upgrade, given the changed design, certainly falls short. The once-quite chiseled Datejust now appears slightly rounded in many places, giving it a much more pleasing effect, but without any loss of seriousness. The new bracelets, the sporty Oyster or the small-link, elegant Jubilé, offer much more wearing comfort compared to their predecessors, with a much easier-to-handle clasp. For the masters of creation, the culmination is certainly the Datejust II, which meets the general public's desire for larger watches, and comes in a 1-3/5" (41mm) case.

This way, both men and women are always appropriately dressed: on Casual Friday with jeans, on the beach in bathing suits, or at a business meeting in pinstripes. The watch is just as versatile: from 1" to 1-3/5" (26-41mm), sometimes as Lady Datejust or Pearlmaster, sometimes in stainless steel, yellow or rose gold, sometimes decorated with precious stones, but always a chronometer with automatic movement.

The 1-2/5" (37mm) diameter Rolex Oyster Perpetual Datejust is certainly man-oriented while also flattering the ladies. This stainless steel chronometer with white gold bezel ("Rolésor white") also features ten eye-catching diamond hour markers (5,355 euros/$7,226 U.S. dollars).

Prince Rather than Oyster

Rolex is more than the Oyster. In the 1930s, the Swiss made, with great success, the elegant, rectangular Prince, which disappeared from the market at the end of the 1940s. Only in 2005 did Rolex give new life to the idea of an elegant rectangular watch.

Rolex Prince Brancard Chronometer "Extra Prima Observatory Quality" Ref. 971 U from 1935. An auctioneer's estimate: about 14,000 euros/$18,855 U.S. dollars.

For decades, the "Prince" had existed alongside the "Oyster" in the collection, and was offered as an alternative for all those who did not have to own either a waterproof or automatic watch. The Prince successfully set its face against the spirit of the times, which, already at the end of the 1930s, called for round or at least cushion-shaped watches. At the same time, the Prince was no "starter model," but usually much more expensive than a comparable manually-wound Oyster.

When the first Prince came on the market in 1928, rectangular wristwatches were a symbol of modernity: their external shape demonstrated that this was no "old hat" converted ladies' pocket watch. Rectangular watch movements such as the Aegler Caliber 877, which mutated in 1932, with some modifications, into the Caliber "T.S. Ref. 300," and ticked in the Prince, were new designs per se. The rectangular Rolex underlined the brand's high quality standards with chronometer certification ("certified precision"), sometimes with a certificate from the Kew Observatory. A separate second hand was mandatory because it made the precision both demonstrable and comprehensible. This feature was also popular among medical professionals who wanted to measure patient's pulses, which is why the Prince was often referred to as the "Doctor's Watch." The time display, with hour and minute hands, migrated to the upper half of the rectangular dial and could be read in one glance.

The same goes for the new edition of the annotated rectangular watch from 2005, but otherwise the new Prince is much more than a citation of the old virtues — it is the new interpretation of a philosophy that broadly transcends the rectangular design, the manual-winding movement, and the divided dial. If you consider the minimal development of the Oyster models in the last fifty years, you would be aware of the consequences of the decision to bring out the legendary "Prince" anew, in the Cellini collection.

It has become bigger, bulkier, wider, higher, and heavier. This is also the only concession that the developers of the Rolex Prince were ready to make to modern contemporary taste. This traditional model has preserved the elegance for which it was revered and sought-after until far beyond the end of production in the 1950s. What is remarkable is the fact that the typical Art Deco-style elements, like engine-turning, fluting, and curved edges, still create their effect even today.

A Prince with Four Faces

In 2013, the new Prince came on the market in four different models — yes, "models," because the distinctive features go far beyond case material and dial color.

The Prince operates under Reference number 5440/8, with smoothly-curved yellow gold case, sunray design-engraved sides, and a "Clous de Paris" (hobnail pattern) decoration on the dial. The pyramid-shaped "hobnails" are mechanically carved out of solid gold plate; the two areas for the time and small second hand displays are smooth finished. This engine-turning pattern is also found on the entire movement plate, open to view for the first time via a Rolex display back, which, as shown, also has a style function.

Rolex Prince Ref. 5442/5 in rose gold with "Rayon Flammé de la Gloire" (flaming rays of glory) decoration on dial and movement surfaces.

Rolex Prince Ref. 5440/8 in yellow gold with hobnail, engine-turning pattern.

Rolex Prince Ref. 5441/9 in white gold with fluted case.

Rolex Prince Ref. 5443/9 in white gold with graphically-designed dial.

The fact that the new Caliber 7040 involves a contemporary Rolex design is already clear from the solid bridge over the regulator-less balance with Microstella adjustment weights. Despite the typical watch-hand mechanism with decentralized hour and minute hand axis and "isolated" small second, it has no relationship to the legendary Caliber T.S. Ref. 300, which was made by watch movement manufacturer Aegler in Biel (later the Rolex in-house manufacture). The new Rolex manual-winding movement is solidly dimensioned and perhaps does not have as elegant an effect as you might be accustomed to from other Geneva in-house watches. Therefore, the barrel cover proudly bears the laser-engraved inscription "chronometer" — something not available with any other shaped movement, either from Geneva or anywhere else.

Reference 5441/9 has a smooth-surface white gold case with striped fluted hoods between the band lugs. Its dial is decorated with concentric, engine-turning grooves around the main scale, and this pattern is also repeated on the movement plate here with the balance as the "epicenter." The effect is stunning and certainly needs some getting used to, but, on the other hand, a great brand like Rolex can certainly set its own aesthetic standards.

Under the Reference number 5442/5, lies a Prince in a curved rose-gold case with stepped sides and "waisted" back, which emphasizes the curvature. In reality, this back is flat, like the sapphire crystal that it holds, which is simply pressed, not screwed, into place. The blackened dial has a subtle sunburst pattern radiating from the center of the small second hand and is flanked by two fluted borders under the crystal.

The finishing pattern on the movement appears to arise from the balance staff and, with its charcoal gray gleam, offers a sporty look on the gracefully-curved train wheel cocks, despite all the elegance. The Reference 5443/9 dial is also decorated with sunburst or flaming rays, but here the two scales are graphically extended to the corners of the bezel, which gives the watch a modernist 1960s-

The new Prince is now in the Cellini collection.

Rolex Caliber 7040-1 in yellow gold finish with engine-turning, hobnail pattern.

style expression. The white-gold case is soft and fluid, however, with a pronounced wavy ribbing along the sides. The sunburst pattern creates an almost psychedelic effect on the movement surface, since the rays emanate from two different centers (intermediate and center wheels) and intersect at a chink between two train wheel cocks.

A Good Bequest

Those concessionaires who were treated to a small presentation at the watch and jewelry fair, BaselWorld, showed great interest in the new Rolex Prince, with its from-the-ground-up newly developed shaped movement Caliber 7040 (by the way, depending on the model and surface finishing, denoted with an additional 1, 2, 3, or 4). Prices are as you might expect — 11,000 euros ($14,816 U.S.) for the two white gold models and 10,500 euros ($14,142 U.S.) for the red or yellow gold References — not exactly any special offer, yet these solid cases are certainly something difficult to accomplish. At the same time, Rolex sets its own standards, not only in aesthetics, but also for the pricing structure for such an in-house manual-winding shaped movement piece, with chronometer certificates.

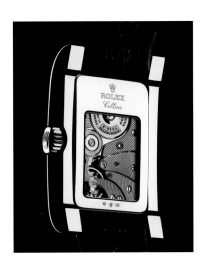

Rolex Caliber 7040-3 with engine-turning, concentric, groove pattern.

Rolex Caliber 7040-4 with decorative sunburst finish.

*Model-
Overview*

1924
Oyster "For All Climates"

Case:
Yellow gold, 9-carat, screw-down back, leather strap, 1-1/5" x 1-3/10" (32x34mm)

Watch Movement:
Rhodium-plated, 6 adj., manual winding

Remarks:
This rare Oyster made it apparent by its name "For All Climates" that it was intended for all climatic conditions.

Estimated Value: Euro 2,000 ($2,695 U.S.)

1935
Oyster "Channel Swimmer's Watch"

Reference: 3224

Case:
Silver, screw-down back, leather strap, 1-3/10" (33mm)

Watch Movement:
Rhodium-plated, manual winding

Remarks:
This watch, also called the "Channel Swimmer," commemorates Mercedes Gleitze's swim across the English Channel in 1927 with a Rolex Oyster on her wrist. Until that time, this was the most impressive endurance test for a waterproof watch.

Estimated Value: Euro 2,000 ($2,695 U.S.)

1937
Men's watch

Reference: 3139

Case:
Stainless steel, screw-down back, leather strap, 1-1/10" x 1-2/5" (29x37mm)

Watch Movement:
Rhodium-plated, decorated, manual winding

Remarks:
Rare men's watch in cushion-shaped case

Estimated Value: Euro 2,000 ($2,695 U.S.)

1940
Oyster Chronometer Viceroy

Reference: 3359

Case:
Stainless steel/red gold, 1-1/10" x 1-1/2" (29x38mm), three-part, screw-down back, stainless steel/red gold link bracelet

Watch Movement:
Nickel-plated, smoothed, polished screws, "patented Super Balance," 17 jewels, 7 adj.

Remarks:
Extremely rare Oyster Viceroy in bi-colored case; the movement has the patented "Super Balance"

Estimated Value: Euro 4,000 ($5,388 U.S.)

1943
"Radiomir" Panerai

Reference: 3646

Case:
Stainless steel, screw-down back, leather strap, 1-4/5" (47mm)

Watch Movement:
Rhodium-plated, with "Geneva stripe" decoration, chatoned, signed: "Rolex 17 Rubis," 17 jewels, manual winding

Remarks:
Important watch used by frog-men of the Italian Navy; it was offered with original leather strap

Estimated Value: Euro 40,000 ($53,880 U.S.)

1938
Officine Panerai "Brevet-tato"

Prototype Frogman's Watch

Reference: 3646

Case:
Stainless steel, screw-down back, leather strap, 1-4/5" (47mm)

Watch Movement:
Rhodium-plated, with "Geneva stripe" decoration, chatoned, manual winding

Remarks:
Important watch used by frog-men of the Italian Navy. This watch is a prototype, made only for presentation purposes. The case back is signed "Oyster Watch Geneva Swiss."

Estimated Value: Euro 70,000 ($94,325 U.S.)

1941
Oyster Raleigh

Reference: 3478

Case:
Stainless steel, screw-down back, leather strap, 1-1/10" x 1-2/5" (29x37mm)

Watch Movement:
Rhodium-plated, manual winding

Remarks:
Rare Oyster Raleigh

Estimated Value: Euro 1,400 ($1,885 U.S.)

1966
Oyster Precision
"California Dial"

Reference: 6424

Case:
Stainless steel, screw-down back, leather strap, 1-2/5" (36mm)

Watch Movement:
Rhodium-plated, manual winding

Remarks:
Extremely rare Oyster with "California" dial. The watch was offered with the original box and certificate.

Estimated Value: Euro 3,500 ($4,714.50 U.S.)

1930
Prince Railway Jumping Hours
"Observatory Quality"

Reference: 1587HS

Case:
Red/white 18-carat gold, snap-in back, leather strap, 9/10" x 1-3/5" (23x42mm)

Watch Movement:
Rhodium-plated, 6 adj., manual winding

Remarks:
Rare men's watch in a stepped-side, rectangular case with jumping, digital hour display and small second hand

Estimated Value: Euro 20,000 ($26,938 U.S.)

1935
Prince Chronometer

Case:
Yellow 18-carat gold, snap-in back, leather strap, 4/5" x 1-1/2" (20x40mm)

Watch Movement:
Rhodium-plated, 8 adj., manual winding

Remarks:
Elegant "Prince Classic"

Estimated Value: Euro 4,500 ($6,061.50 U.S.)

1936
Prince Railway "Observatory Quality"

Reference: 1527M

Case:
White/yellow 18-carat gold, snap-in back, leather strap, 4/5" x 1-3/5" (22x42mm)

Watch Movement:
Rhodium-plated, 15 jewels, 6 adj., manual winding

Remarks:
Rare Prince Railway in perfect condition with movement in Observatory quality

Estimated Value: Euro 12,000 ($16,164 U.S.)

1935
Prince Brancard Chronometer
"Observatory Quality"

Case:
White/yellow 18-carat gold, snap-in back, leather strap, 1" x 1-7/10" (26x43mm)

Watch Movement:
Caliber 971, rhodium-plated, 6 adj., manual winding

Remarks:
Rare Prince Brancard chronometer with a movement in Observatory quality

Estimated Value: Euro 22,000 ($29,645 U.S.)

1945
Prince Brancard Chronometer Jumping Hours "Extra Prima Observatory Quality"

Reference: 1491

Case:
White 9-carat gold, snap-in back, leather strap, 9/10" x 1-7/10" (25x43mm)

Watch Movement:
Rhodium-plated, 6 adj., manual winding

Remarks:
Rare chronometer with digital jumping hour display; this watch was offered with original box and rating certificate from the Biel Observatory

Estimated Value: Euro 30,000 ($40,410 U.S.)

1950
Prince Aerodynamic Chronometer

Reference: 3361

Case:
18-carat rose gold, 7/10" x 1-4/5" (19x46mm), two-piece, snap-in back, leather strap

Watch Movement:
Caliber 310, rhodium-plated, smoothed, polished screws, Quality "Ultra Prima," 18 jewels, 6 adj.

Remarks:
Asymmetric Prince, "Aerodynamic," introduced in 1939. Diminishing case thickness in profile. The Caliber 310 was manufactured from 1932-38, but also installed in the later Ultra Prima-quality Prince models. This watch was offered with an 18-carat Rolex pin buckle.

Estimated Value: Euro 10,000 ($13,475 U.S.)

1932
Oyster Perpetual Chronometer

Made for Ronchi, Milan

Reference: 3347

Case:
Red 18-carat gold, screw-down back, Leather strap, 1-1/10" (29mm)

Watch Movement:
Rhodium-plated, automatic

Remarks:
Extremely rare, early Oyster with double hour index markings; the markers on the bezel, the "iii," and the "ix" are set vertically while they are horizontal on the watch dial. The watch has a rare double signature "Ronchi Milano."

Estimated Value: Euro 10,000 ($13,475 U.S.)

1939
Oyster Perpetual Chronometer

Reference: 3348

Case:
Stainless steel, screw-down back, leather strap, 1-1/10" (29mm)

Watch Movement:
Rhodium-plated, automatic

Remarks:
Extremely rare Oyster chronometer with a very wide bezel

Estimated Value: Euro 2,000 ($2,695 U.S.)

121

1932
Oyster Perpetual Super Precision

Reference: 3353

Case:
Stainless steel/gold, screw-down back, stainless steel link bracelet, 1-1/10" (29mm)

Watch Movement:
Rhodium-plated, automatic

Remarks:
Extremely rare, early automatic Oyster with small second hand

Estimated Value: Euro 8,000 ($10,775 U.S.)

1938
Oyster Perpetual Chronometer Bubble Back "Hooded Lugs"

Case:
Stainless steel/gold, screw-down back, leather strap, 1-1/5" (32mm)

Watch Movement:
Rhodium-plated, automatic

Remarks:
Oyster Perpetual with Roman numerals and case with hooded band lugs

Estimated Value: Euro 4,500 ($6,063.75 U.S.)

1946
Presidential Seal

Reference: 6085

Case:
14-carat yellow gold, 1-3/10" (33mm), two-part, screw-down back, leather strap

Watch Movement:
Nickel-plated, decorated, polished screws, automatic winding rotor

Remarks:
"The great seal of the United States." Important Oyster with an enamel hotnail dial by C. Poluzzi. Due to the complex hand-workmanship, this watch has the status of a unique piece.

Estimated Value: Euro 100,000 ($134,750 U.S.)

1948
Oyster Perpetual Chronometer

Reference: 3372

Case:
18-carat yellow gold, 1-1/5" (32mm), three-part, screw-down back, 18-carat Oyster gold link bracelet

Watch Movement:
Rhodium-plated, polished screws, automatic winding rotor

Remarks:
Rare Oyster "Bubble Back" chronometer with lavender-colored enamel dial and index bezel. The watch was offered with the original box. This trio (see also the next two pieces, at top right) were custom-made for an Indian customer.

Estimated Value: Mixed lot Euro 16,000 ($21,560 U.S.)

1948
Oyster Perpetual
Chronometer

Reference: 3131

Case:
18-carat yellow gold, 1-1/5"
(32mm), three-part, screw-
down back, 18-carat Oyster
gold link bracelet

Watch Movement:
Rhodium-plated, polished
screws, automatic winding
rotor

Remarks:
Rare automatic "Bubble Back"
chronometer with blue enamel
dial; the watch was offered in the original jewelry case

Estimated Value: Mixed lot Euro 16,000
($21,560 U.S.)

1949
Oyster Perpetual
Chronometer

Reference: 3131

Case:
18-carat yellow gold, 1-1/5"
(32mm), three-part, screw-
down back, 18-carat Oyster
gold link bracelet

Watch Movement:
Rhodium-plated, polished
screws, automatic winding
rotor

Remarks:
Rare Oyster chronometer with
green enamel dial; the watch
was offered in the original
jewelry case

Estimated Value: Mixed lot Euro 16,000
($21,560 U.S.)

1948
Oyster Perpetual
Bubble Back

Reference: 3133

Case:
Stainless steel, screw-down
back, gold bezel, stainless
steel/gold link bracelet, 1-1/5"
(32mm)

Watch Movement:
Rhodium-plated, automatic

Remarks:
Oyster "Bubble Back" with
very readable, large luminous
numerals

Estimated Value: Euro 4,000
($5,388 U.S.)

1949
Oyster Perpetual
Chronometer
with "Mickey Mouse" dial

Reference: 3131

Case:
14-carat rose gold, screw-
down back, leather strap,
1-1/5" (32mm)

Watch Movement:
Rhodium-plated, automatic

Remarks:
Rare Oyster Perpetual with
original "Mickey Mouse" dial;
the watch was offered with the
original box and Rolex buckle

Estimated Value: Euro 10,000
($13,475 U.S.)

1949
Oyster Perpetual Chronometer
"California Dial"

Reference: 5013

Case:
Stainless steel, screw-down back, red gold bezel, 1-1/5" x 1-1/2" (32x39mm)

Watch Movement:
Rhodium-plated, automatic

Remarks:
Rare Oyster with original "California" dial (half Roman, half Arab numerals) and small second hand

Estimated Value: Euro 3,500 ($4,726.40 U.S.)

1949
Oyster Perpetual Chronometer Bubble Back
"Hooded Lugs"

Reference: 3065

Case:
Stainless steel/gold, screw-down back, bi-color link bracelet, 1-1/5" x 1-1/2" (32x40mm)

Watch Movement:
Rhodium-plated, automatic

Remarks:
Extremely rare "Bubble Back" with hooded band lugs and original "California" dial (half Roman, half Arabic numerals); the watch was offered with the original box

Estimated Value: Euro 6,000 ($8,081 U.S.)

1953
Oyster Perpetual
Precision Explorer

Reference: 6150

Case:
Stainless steel, screw-down back, leather strap, 1-3/10" (35mm)

Watch Movement:
Rhodium-plated, automatic

Remarks:
Early Explorer model

Estimated Value: Euro 5,500 ($7,427 U.S.)

1953
Oyster Perpetual
Chronometer Explorer

Reference: 6350

Case:
Stainless steel, screw-down back, leather strap, 1-3/10" (35mm)

Watch Movement:
Rhodium-plated, automatic

Remarks:
Rare early Explorer model with textured dial

Estimated Value: Euro 7,000 ($9,452 U.S.)

1956
Oyster Explorer
officially certified Chronometer

Reference: 6610

Case:
Stainless steel, 1-2/5" (36mm),
three-part, screw-down back,
leather strap

Watch Movement:
Caliber 1030, rhodium-plated,
smoothed, polished screws,
automatic winding rotor, 25 jewels,
6 adj.

Remarks:
Rare Oyster Perpetual Chronometer
with white dial.

Estimated Value: Euro 15,000
($20,203.50 U.S.)

1958
Oyster Perpetual Explorer
Super Precision

Reference: 5500

Case:
Stainless steel, screw-down
back, stainless steel link
bracelet,
1-3/10" (34mm)

Watch Movement:
Caliber 1530, rhodium-plated,
automatic

Remarks: Rare Explorer

Estimated Value: Euro 4,000
($5,401.60 U.S.)

1960
Oyster Perpetual Precision
Explorer Date

Reference: 5700

Case:
Stainless steel, screw-down
back, gold bezel, stainless steel
link bracelet, 1-3/10" (35mm)

Watch Movement:
Caliber 1530, rhodium-plated,
25 jewels, automatic

Remarks:
Extremely rare Oyster Explorer
Date for the Canadian market

Estimated Value: Euro 3,500
($4,716 U.S.)

1984
Explorer II

Reference: 16550

Case:
Stainless steel, 1-1/2" (39mm),
three-part, screw-down back,
stainless steel link bracelet

Watch Movement:
Caliber 3085, rhodium-plated,
smoothed, mirror-polished
screws, automatic winding
rotor, 27 jewels, 6 adj.

Remarks:
Explorer II with rare cream-
colored dial; the watch was
sold with a guarantee

Estimated Value: Euro 7,500
($10,101.75 U.S.)

1954
Star Dial

Reference: 6098

Case:
18-carat yellow gold, 1-3/10"
(35mm), two-part, screw-down
back, leather strap

Watch Movement:
Red gold-plated, polished
screws, automatic winding
rotor, 25 jewels

Remarks:
Big "Bubble Back" in an
exceptional combination with
case with textured "Hon-
eycomb" dial. This has the
extremely rare applied golden
star index markers. The watch was offered with an 18-carat
gold Rolex pin buckle in the original case.

Estimated Value: Euro 20,000
($27,008 U.S.)

1952
Oyster Perpetual
Datejust Chronometer

Reference: 6105

Case:
18-carat yellow gold, screw-
down back, leather strap,
1-3/10" (35mm)

Watch Movement:
Rhodium-plated, automatic

Remarks:
Elegant Oyster Datejust in
gold. The watch was offered
with the original certificate
from the Biel Observatory.

Estimated Value: Euro 5,500
($7,411 U.S.)

1955
Oyster Perpetual Datejust
Superlative Chronometer
"Serpico y Laino"

Reference: 6605

Case:
18-carat yellow gold, screw-
down back, leather strap,
1-2/5" (36mm)

Watch Movement:
Caliber 1065, rhodium-plated,
25 jewels, 6 adj., automatic

Remarks:
Oyster with extremely rare dial
imprint "Superlative Chronometer by official test, 50m =
165ft", and a double signature
"Serpico y Laino"

Estimated Value: Euro 5,500
($7,411 U.S.)

1945
Oyster Perpetual
Chronometer

Reference: 4467

Case:
18-carat yellow gold, screw-
down back, leather strap,
1-2/5" (36mm)

Watch Movement:
Rhodium-plated, automatic

Remarks:
Elegant Oyster in gold case

Estimated Value: Euro 8,000
($10,775 U.S.)

1955
Datejust Chronometer

Reference: 6305/1

Case:
Stainless steel, screw-down back, stainless steel link bracelet, 1-2/5" (36mm)

Watch Movement:
Caliber 745, rhodium-plated, automatic

Remarks:
Rare Datejust with engine-turning dial, black/red date display, and white gold bezel; this model was only produced from 1953–55

Estimated Value: Euro 3,500 ($4,726 U.S.)

1956
Date Chronometer

Reference: 1503

Case:
18-carat yellow gold, screw-down back, Milanese bracelet, 1-3/10" (34mm)

Watch movement:
Caliber 1560, rhodium-plated, decorated, 26 jewels, 6 adj., automatic

Remarks:
Rolex Date with double signature Rolex and "Serpico y Laino"

Estimated Value: Euro 4,500 ($6,063.75 U.S.)

1961
Oyster Perpetual Day-Date Chronometer

Reference: 1803

Case:
18-carat yellow gold, screw-down back, leather strap, 1-2/5" (36mm)

Watch movement:
Caliber 1555, rhodium-plated, decorated, 26 jewels, 6 adj., automatic

Remarks:
Men's watch with day and date display

Estimated value: Euro 5,500 ($7,411 U.S.)

1953
Oyster Perpetual Chronometer

Reference: 6084

Case:
18-carat yellow-gold, 1-3/10" (33mm), two-part, screw-down back, 18-carat yellow gold link bracelet

Watch Movement:
Nickel-plated, decorated, polished screws, automatic winding rotor

Remarks:
Golden "Bubble Back" with original Oyster gold link bracelet and index bezel. The watch was offered in the original case.

Estimated Value: Euro 4,000 ($5,401.60 U.S.)

1958
Oyster Perpetual
"Milgauss" Superlative
Chronometer
"officially certified"

Reference: 6541

Case:
Stainless steel, screw-down
back, rotating bezel, stainless steel link bracelet, 1-2/5"
(36mm)

Watch Movement:
Caliber 1066M, rhodium-plated 25 jewels, 6 adj., automatic

Remarks:
Extremely rare first generation
Milgauss, still without "light-
ning flash hand"

Estimated Value: Euro 50,000
($67,375 U.S.)

1966
Oyster Perpetual
"Milgauss"

Reference: 1019

Case:
Stainless steel, screw-down
back, stainless steel link bracelet, 1-2/5" (37mm)

Watch movement:
Rhodium-plated, automatic

Remarks:
Rare early Milgauss — the
watch movement is surround-
ed by a soft iron protective
cover, thus protected from
magnetism up to 1,000 gauss.

Estimated Value: Euro 20,000
($27,008 U.S.)

1972
Oyster Perpetual
Datejust Chronometer
"Thunderbird"

Reference: 1625

Case:
18-carat yellow gold, screw-
down back, leather strap,
1-2/5" (36mm)

Watch Movement:
Caliber 1570, rhodium-plated,
automatic

Remarks:
Early "Thunderbird" in gold

Estimated Value: Euro 4,500
($6,063.75 U.S.)

1977
Oyster Perpetual
Datejust Chronometer
"Thunderbird"

Reference: 1625

Case:
Stainless steel, screw-down
back, 18-carat, gold bezel,
1-2/5" (36mm)

Watch Movement:
Rhodium-plated, automatic

Remarks:
Rare Oyster "Thunderbird"
with black dial

Estimated Value: Euro 3,000
($4,051 U.S.)

1954
Oyster Perpetual
Turn-O-Graph

Reference: 6202

Case:
Stainless steel, 1-2/5″ (36mm),
three-part, rotatable bezel,
screw-down back, leather strap

Watch Movement:
Nickel-plated, smoothed,
polished screws, automatic
winding rotor

Remarks:
Early Oyster Turn-O-Graph
with rotating black index bezel

Estimated Value: Euro 4,500
($6,063.75 U.S.)

1956
Oyster Perpetual
GMT Master Chronometer
"officially certified"

Reference: 6542

Case:
Stainless steel, screw-down
back, rotating bezel, stainless steel link bracelet, 1-1/2″
(38mm)

Watch Movement:
Caliber 1030, rhodium-plated,
25 jewels, 6 adj., automatic

Remarks:
This watch has the original
acrylic rotatable bezel; a second time zone can be set with
the 24-hour hand and bezel

Estimated Value: Euro 15,000
($20,256 U.S.)

1966
Oyster Perpetual
GMT Master

Reference: 1675

Case:
18-carat yellow gold, screw-
down back, rotating bezel,
gold link bracelet, 1-1/2″
(39mm)

Watch Movement:
Rhodium-plated, automatic

Remarks:
Golden GMT Master with 24-
hour display; the rotating bezel
can be used to set a second
time zone

Estimated Value: Euro 20,000
($27,008 U.S.)

1958
Oyster Perpetual GMT
Master
"Pan Am" Chronometer
"officially certified"

Reference: 6542

Case:
Stainless steel, screw-down
back, rotating bezel, stainless steel link bracelet, 1-1/2″
(38mm)

Watch Movement:
Caliber 1035, rhodium-plated,
25 jewels, 6 adj., automatic

Remarks:
Extremely rare GMT-Master,
launched as a special series
for Pan Am; fewer than 200 pieces were made for this special
series

Estimated Value: Euro 20,000
($27,008 U.S.)

1955
Oyster Perpetual
Submariner
"James Bond"

Reference: 6205

Case:
Stainless steel, screw-down back, stainless steel link bracelet, 1-2/5" (36mm)

Watch Movement:
Caliber A260, rhodium-plated, automatic

Remarks:
This watch got its nickname from its appearance in several early "James Bond" films.

Estimated Value: Euro 10,000 ($13,469 U.S.)

1958
Oyster Perpetual
Submariner 200 m/660 ft
"James Bond"

Reference: 6538

Case:
Stainless steel, screw-down back, stainless steel link bracelet, 1-2/5" (37mm)

Watch movement:
Caliber 1030, rhodium-plated, 25 jewels, automatic

Remarks:
This Submariner owes its nickname to its appearance in several early "James Bond" films.

Estimated Value: Euro 25,000 ($33,760 U.S.)

1957
Oyster Perpetual
Submariner 100 m/330 ft

Reference: 6536/1

Case:
Stainless steel, screw-down back, rotating bezel, stainless steel link bracelet, 1-2/5" (37mm)

Watch Movement:
Caliber 1030, rhodium-plated, 25 jewels, 6 adj., automatic

Remarks:
Early Submariner, chronometer version

Estimated Value: Euro 9,000 ($12,122 U.S.)

1959
Oyster Perpetual
Submariner
"Officially
certified Chronometer"

Reference: 6538

Case:
Stainless steel, screw-down back, rotating bezel, stainless steel link bracelet, 1-1/2" (38mm)

Watch Movement:
Caliber 1030, rhodium-plated, 25 jewels, 6 adj., automatic

Remarks:
Unique Submariner featuring the original, almost unknown dial version, with red depth indicator and red inscription "Officially certified Chronometer"; this so-called "James Bond" model got its name from its use in several early "Bond" films.

Estimated Value: Euro 25,000 ($33,760 U.S.)

1961
Oyster Perpetual
Submariner 100 m/330 ft

Reference: 5508

Case:
Stainless steel, screw-down back, stainless steel link bracelet, 1-2/5" (37mm)

Watch Movement:
Caliber 1530, rhodium-plated, 25 jewels, 6 adj., automatic

Remarks:
Unique Submariner with Explorer dial and notable back engraving "Casma Lima Peru 4/2/63"

Estimated Value: Euro 22,000 ($29,631 U.S.)

1964
Oyster Perpetual
Submariner
"200 m = 660 ft"
Explorer dial

Reference: 5513

Case:
Stainless steel, screw-down back, stainless steel link bracelet, 1-1/2" (39mm)

Watch Movement:
Caliber 1520, rhodium-plated, 26 jewels, 6 adj., automatic

Remarks:
Submariner with extremely rare "Explorer"-style dial

Estimated Value: Euro 20,000 ($27,008 U.S.)

1970
Oyster Perpetual
Submariner

Reference: 5513

Case:
Stainless steel, 1-1/2" (39mm), three-part, rotatable bezel, screw-down back, textile diving watch band

Watch Movement:
Rhodium-plated, smoothed, polished screws, winding rotor, 26 jewels

Remarks:
Extremely rare military frogman's watch for the Royal Navy's "British Special Boat Service"; a distinguishing feature is the original sword hand pictured here, which is particularly easy to read underwater. With this, the watch must have fixed bar lugs.

Estimated Value: Euro 25,000 ($33,760 U.S.)

1978
Oyster Perpetual
Sea-Dweller
Submariner 2000

Reference: 1665

Case:
Stainless steel, screw-down back, rotatable bezel, 1-1/2" (39mm)

Watch Movement:
Caliber 1665, rhodium-plated, automatic

Remarks:
Rare early Sea-Dweller diving watch with red dial imprint; the watch was offered with a Rolex service receipt

Estimated Value: Euro 15,000 ($20,256 U.S.)

131

1950
Perpetual Chronometer
Precision

Reference: 8171

Case:
Stainless steel, screw-down
back, leather strap, 1-1/2"
(38mm)

Watch Movement:
Rhodium-plated, automatic

Remarks:
Extremely rare Oyster with full
calendar, small second hand,
and moon phase display; this
model was only manufac-
tured in a small series and is
very difficult to find. Watch is
number 279.

Estimated Value: Euro 50,000
($67,345 U.S.)

1949
Perpetual Chronometer

Reference: 8171

Case:
18-carat red gold, snap-in
back, leather strap, 1-1/2"
(38mm)

Watch Movement:
Rhodium-plated, automatic

Remarks:
Extremely rare men's watch,
produced in a small series.
This watch (serial number 202)
is almost impossible to find in
red gold. The watch was offered with original case.

Estimated Value: Euro 40,000
($53,876 U.S.)

1953
Oyster Perpetual
Chronometer
"Officially Certified"

Reference: 6062

Case:
Stainless steel, screw-down
back, stainless steel link bracelet, 1-2/5" (36mm)

Watch Movement:
Rhodium-plated, automatic

Remarks:
Extremely rare automatic
Oyster with full calendar and
moon phase display; this
model was manufactured between 1950-53: 350 pieces in
yellow-gold, 50 pieces in red-gold, and in miniscule numbers
in steel

Estimated Value: Euro 90,000
($121,536 U.S.)

1953
Oyster Perpetual
Chronometer

Reference: 6062

Case:
18-carat yellow-gold, 1-3/10"
(35mm), two-part, screw-down
back, leather strap

Watch Movement:
Rhodium-plated, polished
screws, automatic winding
rotor

Remarks:
Important men's watch with
full calendar; date hand, weekday, and day of the month
display windows and Moon phase display by the "6"; only 350
pieces of this model were manufactured between 1950 and
1953

Estimated Value: Euro 70,000
($94,283 U.S.)

1949
Chronograph Date
Compact

Reference: 4768

Case:
Stainless steel, 1-3/10"
(35mm), three-part, snap-in
back, leather strap

Watch Movement:
Caliber 72C, rhodium-plated,
smoothed, with intermediate
wheel control, finely polished,
beveled chronograph steel
parts, mirror-polished screws,
17 jewels

Remarks:
Important rare chronograph
with 30-minute and 12-hour counters, full calendar with date
hands, and windows to display weekday and month; just 220
pieces were produced

Estimated Value: Euro 35,000
($47,155.50 U.S.)

1950
Chronograph with
Full Calendar

Reference: 4768

Case:
18-carat rose gold, snap-in
back, leather strap, 1-3/10"
(35mm)

Watch Movement:
Caliber Valjoux 72C, rhodium-plated, with intermediate wheel control, manual
winding

Remarks:
Rare rose gold chronograph
with 30-minute and 12-hour
counters, full calendar, and
tachymeter scale

Estimated Value: Euro 35,000
($47,155 U.S.)

1954
Oyster Chronograph
Anti-magnetic
"Jean-Claude Killy"

Reference: 6036

Case:
Stainless steel, screw-down
back, stainless steel link bracelet, 1-2/5" (36mm)

Watch Movement:
Caliber 72C, rhodium-plated,
with column wheel control,
manual winding

Remarks:
Rare chronograph with
30-minute and 12-hour counters, as well as full calendar
with date, weekday, and month; model named after the same-
named alpine ski racer

Estimated Value: Euro 70,000
($94,283 U.S.)

1953
Oyster Chronograph

Reference: 6236

Case:
18-carat yellow gold, 1-2/5"
(36mm), three-part, screw-
down back, leather strap

Watch Movement:
Caliber 72C, rhodium-plated,
smoothed, with intermedi-
ate wheel control, finely
smoothed, beveled steel
chronograph parts, mirror-
polished screws

Remarks:
Extremely rare chronograph
with 30-minute and 12-hour
counters, full calendar with date hand, and window display for
weekday and month; this is the so-called "Jean-Claude Killy,"
of which 170 pieces were made in yellow-gold

Estimated Value: Euro 80,000
($108,032 U.S.)

133

1932
Military Anti-magnetic Chronograph

Reference: 2508

Case:
Stainless steel, 1-3/10"
(35mm), three-part, snap-in
back, leather strap

Watch movement:
Nickel-plated, smoothed, with
column wheel control, finely-
smoothed chronograph steel
parts, polished screws

Remarks:
Rare chronograph with
30-minute counter; it is one of
the first chronograph models
Rolex produced

Estimated Value: Euro 30,000
($40,512 U.S.)

1935
Chronograph

Reference: 3371

Case:
18-carat yellow gold, 1-3/10"
(35mm), three-part, snap-in
back, leather strap

Watch Movement:
Nickel-plated, smoothed, with
column wheel control, finely
smoothed chronograph steel
parts, polished screws, 17
jewels

Remarks:
Rare, very fine chronograph
with 30-minute counter, tachymeter, and blue telemeter
scales. The watch was offered with a gold Rolex pin buckle.

Estimated Value: Euro 17,000
($22,956 U.S.)

1934
Chronograph
Anti-Magnetic

Reference: 2508

Case:
Yellow 18-carat gold, snap-in
back, leather strap, 1-2/5"
(36mm)

Watch Movement:
Not specified, rhodium-plated,
with column wheel control,
manual winding

Remarks:
One of the first Rolex-pro-
duced, with 30-minute counter
and tachymeter scale

Estimated Value: Euro 16,000
($21,606 U.S.)

1934
Chronograph
Anti-Magnetic

Reference: 3834

Case:
Yellow 18-carat gold, snap-in
back, leather strap, 1-1/5"
(32mm)

Watch Movement:
Not specified, rhodium-plated,
manual winding

Remarks:
Extremely rare chronograph
with 30-minute counter and
additional tachymeter scale

Estimated Value: Euro 12,000
($16,204 U.S.)

1947
Oyster Chronograph

Reference: 4500

Case:
Stainless steel, screw-down back, leather strap, 1-2/5" (36mm)

Watch Movement:
R23, rhodium-plated, with column wheel control, manual winding

Remarks:
Rare Oyster Chronograph with 30-minute counter and additional tachymeter scale

Estimated Value: Euro 20,000 ($27,008 U.S.)

1945
Chronograph
Anti-Magnetic

Reference: 3525

Case:
18-carat yellow gold, screw-down back, leather strap, 1-3/10" (35mm)

Watch Movement:
Rhodium-plated, with column wheel control, manual winding

Remarks:
One of the first Rolex-manufactured Oyster Chronographs from 1945, with 30-minute counter and telemeter scale; this watch was offered with the original jewelry case

Estimated Value: Euro 25,000 ($33,672 U.S.)

1950
Chronograph
Anti-Magnétique

Case:
Yellow 18-carat gold, snap-in back, leather strap, 1-1/5" (30mm)

Watch Movement:
Nickel-plated, with column wheel control, manual winding

Remarks:
Extremely rare chronograph with 30-minute counter and additional tachymeter scale

Estimated Value: Euro 12,000 ($16,204 U.S.)

1948
Chronograph

Reference: 4099

Case:
Stainless steel, snap-in back, leather strap, 1-3/10" (35mm)

Watch Movement:
Rhodium-plated, with column wheel control, manual winding

Remarks:
Rare chronograph in stainless steel with striking band lugs

Estimated Value: Euro 15,000 ($20,256 U.S.)

1965
Chronograph
("Pre-Daytona")

Case:
14-carat yellow gold, screw-down back 1-2/5" (36mm)

Watch Movement:
Rhodium-plated, with column wheel control, manual winding

Remarks:
Blue tachymeter scale

Estimated Value: Euro 38,000 ($51,197 U.S.)

1966
Chronograph
("Pre-Daytona")

Reference: 6238

Case:
Stainless steel, screw-down back, stainless steel link bracelet, 1-2/5" (36mm)

Watch Movement:
Caliber 722.1, rhodium-plated, with column wheel control, 17 jewels, 3 adj., manual winding

Remarks:
Chronograph with 30-minute and 12-hour counters

Estimated Value: Euro 21,000 ($28,284 U.S.)

1965
Chronograph
("Pre-Daytona")

Reference: 6238

Case:
14-carat yellow gold, screw-down back, yellow gold link bracelet, 1-1/5" (32mm)

Watch Movement:
Caliber 72B, rhodium-plated, with column wheel control, manual winding

Remarks:
Chronograph with 30-minute and 12-hour counters

Estimated Value: Euro 50,000 ($67,345 U.S.)

1960
Oyster Cosmograph
Daytona "Paul Newman"

Reference: 6240

Case:
Stainless steel, screw-down back, stainless steel link bracelet, 1-2/5" (37mm)

Watch Movement:
Rhodium-plated, with column wheel control, manual winding

Remarks:
Rare "Daytona" Chronograph with black tachymeter scale on the bezel; the watch was offered with service receipt and certificate of originality

Estimated Value: Euro 40,000 ($53,876 U.S.)

**1967
Oyster Cosmograph
Daytona "Paul Newman"**

Reference: 6239

Case:
Stainless steel, screw-down
back, stainless steel link bracelet, 1-2/5" (36mm)

Watch Movement:
Not specified, with column
wheel control, manual winding

Remarks:
"Daytona" Chronograph "Paul
Newman"; the watch was
offered with original case and
certificate

Estimated Value: Euro 40,000
($53,876 U.S.)

**1968
Oyster Cosmograph
Daytona**

Reference: 6239/6263

Case:
Stainless steel, screw-down
back, stainless steel link
bracelet, 1-2/5" (37mm)

Watch Movement:
Caliber 727, rhodium-plated,
with column wheel control,
manual winding

Remarks:
Rare "Cosmograph" with
30-minute and 12-hour
counters and additional tachymeter scale on the bezel

Estimated Value: Euro 18,000
($24,307 U.S.)

**1977
Oyster Superlative
Chronometer
Cosmograph Daytona**

Reference: 6263

Case:
18-carat yellow gold, 1-1/2"
(38mm), three-part, screw-
down back, 18-carat yellow
gold link bracelet

Watch Movement:
Caliber 727/1531, rhodium-
plated, smoothed, with
intermediate wheel control,
finely polished, beveled Chronograph steel parts, 17 jewels,
3 adj.

Remarks:
Rare chronograph with 30-minute and 12-hour counters; on
the black bezel is a tachymeter scale; crown and pushers are
screw-down. The watch was offered with the original jewel
case and certificate.

Estimated Value: Euro 30,000
($40,419 U.S.)

**1980
Cosmograph**

Reference: 6265

Case:
18-carat yellow-gold, screw-
down back, leather strap,
1-2/5" (37mm)

Watch Movement:
Caliber 722, rhodium-plated,
with column wheel control,
manual winding

Remarks:
Rare "Cosmograph" with
30-minute and 12-hour
counters and additional tachymeter scale on the bezel

Estimated Value: Euro
28,000 ($37,811 U.S.)

137

Oyster Perpetual Datejust

Reference: 116200

Watch Movement:
Automatic, Rolex Caliber
3135, diameter 1-1/10"
(28.5mm), height 1/5"
(6mm), 31 jewels, Breguet
overcoil spring, Glucydur
balance with Microstella
adjustment screws; certified
chronometer

Features:
Hours, minutes, central second hand, date

Case:
Stainless steel, diameter
1-2/5" (36mm), height 2/5"
(11.8mm), sapphire crystal with magnifier over date display;
screw-down crown, waterproof to 10 bar

Bracelet:
Oyster stainless steel with folding clasp and extension

Options:
With jubilé bracelet, different dial styles

Price: Euro 4,220
($5,698 U.S.)

Oyster Perpetual Datejust

Reference: 116201

Watch Movement:
Automatic, Rolex Caliber 3135,
diameter 1-1/10" (28.5mm),
height 1/5" (6mm); 31 jewels,
Breguet overcoil spring, Glucydur balance with Microstella
adjustment screws, certified
chronometer

Features:
Hours, minutes, central second
hand, date

Case:
Stainless steel, diameter 1-2/5"
(36mm), height 2/5" (11.8mm),
sapphire crystal with magnify-
ing lens over the date display; screwed-down crown; waterproof to 10 bar

Bracelet:
Oyster stainless steel/Everose gold with folding clasp and
extension

Options:
With Jubilé bracelet

Price: Euro 6,580
($8,885 U.S.)

Oyster Perpetual Datejust

Reference: 178240

Watch Movement:
Automatic, Rolex Caliber
2235 (base Rolex 2230),
diameter 4/5" (20mm), height
1/5" (5.95mm), 31 jewels,
Breguet overcoil spring,
Glucydur balance with Mi-
crostella adjustment screws,
certified chronometer

Features:
Hours, minutes, central second hand, date

Case:
Stainless steel, diameter
1-1/5" (31mm), height 2/5"
(10.5mm), sapphire crystal with magnifier over date display;
screw-down crown, waterproof to 10 bar

Bracelet:
Jubilé stainless steel, folding clasp

Options:
With Oyster bracelet, various dial styles

Price: Euro 3,920
($5,279 U.S.)

Oyster Perpetual Datejust

Reference: 178245

Watch Movement:
Automatic, Rolex Caliber
2235 (base Rolex 2230),
diameter 4/5" (20mm), height
1/5" (5.95mm), 31 jewels,
Breguet overcoil spring,
Glucydur balance with Mi-
crostella adjustment screws,
certified chronometer

Features:
Hours, minutes, central second hand, date

Case:
Everose gold, diameter
1-1/5" (31mm), height 2/5"
(10.5mm), sapphire crystal with magnifier over the date display; screw-down crown, waterproof to 10 bar

Bracelet:
President Everose gold, folding clasp

Options:
Various dial styles

Price: Euro 17,790
($24,023 U.S.)

Oyster Perpetual Datejust

Reference: 178241

Watch Movement:
Automatic, Rolex Caliber 2235 (base Rolex 2230), diameter 4/5″ (20mm), height 1/5″ (5.95mm), 31 jewels; Breguet overcoil spring, Glucydur balance with Microstella adjustment screws, certified chronometer

Features:
Hours, minutes, central second hand, date

Case:
Stainless steel, diameter 1-1/5″ (31mm), height 2/5″ (10.5mm); bezel in Everose gold, sapphire crystal with magnifier over date display; screw-down crown; waterproof to 10 bar

Bracelet:
Oyster stainless steel/Everose gold, folding clasp with extension

Options:
With Jubilé bracelet

Price: Euro 5,890
($24,023 U.S.)

Oyster Perpetual Datejust

Reference: 116244

Watch Movement:
Automatic, Rolex Caliber 3135, diameter 1-1/10″ (28.5mm), height 1/5″ (6mm), 31 jewels, Breguet overcoil spring, Glucydur balance with Microstella adjustment screws; certified chronometer

Features:
Hours, minutes, central second hand, date

Case:
Stainless steel, diameter 1-2/5″ (36mm), height 2/5″ (11.6mm), bezel in white gold set with diamonds; sapphire crystal with magnifier over date display; screw-down crown; waterproof to 10 bar

Bracelet:
Jubilé stainless steel, folding clasp

Options:
With Oyster bracelet, various dial styles

Price: Euro 8,800
($11,852 U.S.)

Oyster Perpetual Day-Date II

Reference: 218206

Watch Movement:
Automatic, Rolex Caliber 3156 (base Rolex 3135), diameter 1-1/5″ (30.97mm), height 1/5″ (6.47mm), 31 jewels, "Parachrom" Breguet overcoil spring, Glucydur balance with Microstella adjustment screws; "Paraflex" shock absorber, certified chronometer

Features:
Hours, minutes, central second hand, date, week day

Case:
Platinum, diameter 1-3/5″ (41mm), height 2/5″ (11.9mm), sapphire crystal with magnifier over the date display; screw-down crown; waterproof to 10 bar

Bracelet:
President platinum; folding clasp

Options:
Various dial styles

Price: Euro 39,000
($52,529 U.S.)

Oyster Perpetual Day-Date II

Reference: 218239

Watch Movement:
Automatic, Rolex Caliber 3156 (base Rolex 3135), diameter 1-1/5″ (30.97mm), height 1/5″ (6.47mm), 31 jewels; "Parachrom" Breguet overcoil spring; Glucydur balance with Microstella adjustment screws; "Paraflex" shock absorber, certified chronometer

Features:
Hours, minutes, central second hand, date, weekday

Case:
White gold, diameter 1-3/5″ (41mm), height 2/5″ (11.9mm), sapphire crystal with magnifier over date display; screw-down crown; waterproof to 10 bar

Bracelet:
President white gold, folding clasp

Options:
Various dial styles

Price: Euro 23,100
($31,122 U.S.)

Oyster Perpetual Air King

Reference: 114200

Watch Movement:
Automatic, Rolex Caliber 3130
(base Rolex 3135), diameter
1-1/10″ (28.5mm), height 1/5″
(5.85mm), 31 jewels, Breguet
overcoil spring, Glucydur
balance with Microstella
adjustment screws, certified
chronometer

Features:
Hours, minutes, central second
hand

Case:
Stainless steel, diameter
1-3/10″ (34mm), height 2/5″
(11.1mm), sapphire crystal;
screw-down crown; waterproof to 10 bar

Bracelet:
Oyster stainless steel, folding clasp

Options:
Various dial styles

Price: Euro 3,200
($4,311 U.S.)

Oyster Perpetual

Reference: 116000

Watch Movement:
Automatic, Rolex Caliber 3130
(base Rolex 3135), diameter
1-1/10″ (28.5mm), height
1/5″ (5.85mm), 31 jewels,
"Parachrom" Breguet overcoil
spring, balance with Microstella adjustment screws; certified
chronometer (COSC)

Features:
Hours, minutes, central second
hand

Case:
Stainless steel, diameter 1-2/5″
(36mm), height ½″ (13.2mm),
sapphire crystal, screw-down crown, waterproof to 10 bar

Bracelet:
Oyster stainless steel, folding clasp

Options:
Various dial styles

Price: Euro 3,350
($4,523 U.S.)

Oyster Perpetual Date

Reference: 115234

Watch Movement:
Automatic, Rolex Caliber
3135, diameter 1-1/10″
(28.5mm), height 1/5″ (6mm),
31 jewels, Breguet overcoil
spring, Glucydur balance with
Microstella adjustment screws;
certified chronometer

Features:
Hours, minutes, central second
hand, date

Case:
Stainless steel, diameter
1-3/10″ (34mm), height 2/5″
(11.2mm); white gold ribbed
bezel; sapphire crystal with magnifier over date display; screw-
down crown; waterproof to 10 bar

Bracelet:
Oyster stainless steel, folding clasp with extension

Options:
Various dial styles

Price: Euro 4,730
($6,372 U.S.)

Oyster Perpetual Datejust II

Reference: 116333

Watch Movement:
Automatic, Rolex Cali-
ber 3136, diameter 1-1/5″
(30.97mm), height 1/5″
(6.47mm), 31 jewels, "Parachrom" Breguet overcoil
spring, Glucydur balance with
Microstella adjustment screws,
certified chronometer

Features:
Hours, minutes, central second
hand, date

Case:
Stainless steel, diameter 1-3/5″ (41mm), height 2/5″ (11.8mm);
ribbed bezel in yellow gold; sapphire crystal with magnifier
over date display; screw-down crown; waterproof to 10 bar

Bracelet:
Oyster stainless steel/yellow gold, folding clasp with extension

Options:
Various dial styles

Price: Euro 7,280
($9,807 U.S.)

Oyster Perpetual Datejust II

Reference: 116334

Watch Movement:
Automatic, Rolex Caliber 3136, diameter 1-1/5" (30.97mm), height 1/5" (6.47mm), 31 jewels, "Parachrom" Breguet overcoil spring, Glucydur balance with Microstella adjustment screws, certified chronometer (COSC)

Features:
Hours, minutes, central second hand, date

Case:
Stainless steel, diameter 1-3/5" (41mm), height 2/5" (11.8mm); ribbed bezel in white gold, sapphire crystal with magnifier over date display, crown screw-down crown; waterproof to 10 bar

Bracelet:
Oyster stainless steel, folding clasp with extension

Options:
Various dial styles

Price: Euro 5,750
($7,747 U.S.)

Oyster Perpetual Datejust "Turn-O-Graph"

Reference: 116264

Watch Movement:
Automatic, Rolex Caliber 3135, diameter 1-1/10" (28.5mm), height 1/5" (6mm), 31 jewels, Breguet overcoil spring, Glucydur balance with Microstella adjustment screws; certified chronometer (COSC

Features:
Hours, minutes, central second hand, date

Case:
Stainless steel, diameter 1-2/5" (36mm), height 2/5" (11.7mm); ribbed-pattern bezel in white gold, bilateral rotatable with 60-minute intervals; sapphire crystal with magnifier over date display; screw-down crown; waterproof to 10 bar

Bracelet:
Oyster stainless steel, folding clasp with extension

Price: Euro 6,910
($9,310 U.S.)

Oyster Perpetual "Milgauss"

Reference: 116400

Watch Movement:
Automatic, Rolex Caliber 3131 (base Rolex 3135), diameter 1-1/10" (28.5mm), height 1/5" (5.37mm), 31 jewels, "Parachrom" Breguet overcoil spring; certified chronometer (COSC), with soft-iron inner case and dial protected against magnetic fields

Features:
Hours, minutes, central second hand

Case:
Stainless steel, diameter 1-1/2" (40mm), height ½" (13.2mm), sapphire crystal, screw-down crown; waterproof to 10 bar

Bracelet:
Oyster stainless steel, folding clasp with extension

Options:
With green-tinted sapphire crystal, various dial styles

Price: Euro 4,700
($6,332 U.S.)

Oyster Perpetual Datejust

Reference: 81299

Watch Movement:
Automatic, Rolex Caliber 2235 (base caliber 2230); diameter 4/5" (20mm), height 1/5" (5.95mm); 31 jewels, Breguet overcoil spring, balance with Microstella adjustment screws, certified chronometer (COSC)

Features:
Hours, minutes, central second hand, date

Case:
White gold, diameter 1-3/10" (34mm), height 2/5" (10.6mm), diamond-set bezel; sapphire crystal with magnifier; screw-down crown; waterproof to 10 bar

Bracelet:
White gold, folding clasp

Remarks:
Mother-of-pearl dial with 10 diamonds

Price: Euro 32,760
($44,135 U.S.)

141

Prince

Reference: 5443/9

Watch Movement:
Manual winding, Rolex Caliber 7040-2, 21 jewels, 28,800-vph, power reserve 70 hours; Glu-cydur balance with Microstella adjustment screws; engine-turning with dial sunburst pattern; certified chronometer

Features:
Hours, minutes, small second hand

Case:
White gold, 1-4/5" x 1" (46.8x27.6mm), height 2/5" (10mm), sapphire crystal; display case back

Bracelet:
Crocodile leather strap, double-folding clasp

Price: Euro 11,790
($15,879 U.S.)

Oyster Perpetual Submariner Date

Reference: 116613LB

Watch Movement:
Automatic, Rolex Caliber 3135, diameter 1-1/10" (28.5mm), height 1/5" (6mm), 31 jewels, "Parachrom" Breguet overcoil spring; certified chronometer (COSC)

Features:
Hours, minutes, central second hand

Case:
Stainless steel, diameter 1-1/2" (40mm), height 2/5" (12.5mm), bezel in yellow gold, one-sided rotating with 60 minutes; sapphire crystal with magnifier over date display; screw-down crown; waterproof to 30 bar

Bracelet:
Oyster stainless steel/yellow gold, Glidelock folding clasp

Price:
Precious stones: Euro 7,930 ($10,685 U.S.); yellow gold: Euro 20,800 ($28,022 U.S.)

Oyster Perpetual GMT-Master II

Reference: 116713LN

Watch Movement:
Automatic, Rolex Caliber 3186 (base Rolex 3135), diameter 1-1/10" (28.5mm), height 1/5" (6.4mm), 31 jewels, "Parachrom" Breguet overcoil spring, balance with Microstella adjustment screws, certified chronometer

Features:
Hours, minutes, central second hand, date; 24-hour display, second time zone via independently adjustable hour hand

Case:
Stainless steel, diameter 1-1/2" (40mm), height 2/5" (12.1mm), bezel in yellow gold, bilaterally rotating with 24-hour increments; sapphire crystal with magnifier over date display; screw-down crown; waterproof to 10 bar

Bracelet:
Oyster stainless steel/yellow gold, folding clasp with extension

Price: Euro 7,890
($10,631 U.S.)

Oyster Perpetual Sea-Dweller "Deep Sea"

Reference: 116660

Watch Movement:
Automatic, Rolex Caliber 3135, diameter 1-1/10" (28.5mm), height 1/5" (6mm), 31 jewels, "Parachrom" Breguet overcoil spring, Glucydur balance with Microstella adjustment screws, certified chronometer

Features:
Hours, minutes, central second hand, date

Case:
Diameter 1-7/10" (43mm), height 7/10" (17.68mm); unidirectional rotating bezel with ceramic disc (Cerachrom) and 120 increments; titanium case back; screw-down crown, helium valve; waterproof to 390 bar

Bracelet:
Oyster Fliplock bracelet stainless steel, Glidelock folding clasp

Price: Euro 7,100
($9,565 U.S.)

Oyster Perpetual Yacht-Master II Regatta Chronograph

Reference: 116688

Watch movement:
Automatic, Rolex Caliber 4160 (base Rolex 4130), diameter 1-1/5″ (31.2mm), height 3/10″ (8.05mm), 42 jewels, "Parachrom" Breguet overcoil spring, Glucydur balance with Microstella adjustment screws; power reserve about 72 hours; certified chronometer

Features:
Hours, minutes, small second hand, countdown timer with memory

Case:
Yellow gold, diameter 1-3/5″ (42.6mm), height 1/2″ (12.8mm); bezel with ceramic number plate; sapphire crystal; screw-down crown, waterproof to 10 bar

Bracelet:
Oyster yellow gold, folding clasp with extension

Price: Euro 25,690
($34,610 U.S.)

Oyster Perpetual Cosmograph Daytona

Reference: 116509

Watch Movement:
Automatic, Rolex Caliber 4130; diameter 1-1/5″ (30.5mm), height 1/5″ (6.5mm), 44 jewels, "Parachrom" Breguet overcoil spring, power reserve about 72 hours; chronometer

Features:
Hours, minutes, small second hand, chronograph

Case:
White gold, diameter 1-1/2″ (40mm), height 1/2″ (12.8mm); bezel with tachymeter scale; sapphire crystal; screw-down crown and pusher; waterproof to 10 bar

Bracelet:
Oyster white gold, folding clasp with extension

Price: Euro 23,430
($31,565 U.S.)

Oyster Perpetual Cosmograph Daytona

Reference: 116505

Watch Movement:
Automatic, Rolex Caliber 4130; diameter 1-1/5″ (30.5mm), height 1/5″ (6.5mm), 44 jewels, "Parachrom" Breguet overcoil spring, power reserve about 72 hours; chronometer

Features:
Hours, minutes, small second hand, chronograph

Case:
Everose gold, diameter 1-1/2″ (40mm), height 1/2″ (12.8mm); bezel with tachymeter scale; sapphire crystal; screw-down crown and pusher; waterproof to 10 bar

Bracelet:
Oyster Everose gold, folding clasp with extension

Price: Euro 23,450
($31,597 U.S.)

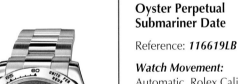

Oyster Perpetual Submariner Date

Reference: *116619LB*

Watch Movement:
Automatic, Rolex Caliber 3135, diameter 1-1/10″ (28.5mm), height 1/5″ (6mm), 31 jewels, Breguet overcoil spring; certified chronometer (COSC)

Features:
Hours, minutes, central second hand, date

Case:
White gold, diameter 1-1/2″ (40mm), height 1/2″ (12.5mm), unilaterally rotating bezel with 120 increments; sapphire crystal; magnifier over the date display; screw-down crown; waterproof to 30 bar

Bracelet:
Oyster white gold, adjustable Glidelock clasp

Price: Euro 22,800
($30,722 U.S.)